LOS ANGELES:graphic design

LOS ANGELES
graphic design

Designed and Edited by
GERRY ROSENTSWIEG

Written by
JULIE PRENDIVILLE

Introduction By
JIM CROSS

Editorial Photography by
ERIC MYER

Published by
MADISON SQUARE PRESS

Copyright 1993 by Madison Square Press
All rights reserved. Copyright under International and
Pan American Copyright Conventions.

No part of this book may be reproduced, stored in a
retrieval system or transmitted in any form, or by any means,
electronic, mechanical, photocopying, recording or other-
wise, without prior permission of the publishers.

While Madison Square Press makes every effort possible
to publish full and correct credits for each work included
in this volume, sometimes errors of omission or commission
may occur. For this we are most regretful, but hereby must
disclaim any liability.

All this book is printed in four color process, a few of the
designs reproduced here may appear to be slightly different
than their original reproduction.

ISBN 0-942604-33-4
Library of Congress Catalog Card Number 92-061446

Distributors to the trade
in the United States & Canada:
Van Nostrand Reinhold
115 Fifth Avenue
New York, NY 10003

Distributed throughout the rest of
the world by:
Hearst Books International
1350 Avenue of the Americas
New York, NY 10019

Publisher:
Madison Square Press
10 East 23rd Street
New York, NY 10010

Editor: Gerry Rosentswieg
Designer: The Graphics Studio

PRINTED IN HONG KONG

End papers reproduced with permission granted by Thomas Bros. Maps.
It is unlawful to copy or reproduce all or any part thereof, whether for personal
use or resale without permission. © Thomas Bros Maps 1993.

CONTENTS

7	Preface
9	Introduction
13	Kimberly Baer Design Associates
21	Baker Design Associates
29	Bass Yager & Associates
37	Besser Joseph Partners
45	Bright & Associates
53	Michael Brock Design
61	Margo Chase Design
69	Coy, Los Angeles
77	Curry Design
85	The Designory, Inc.
93	Rod Dyer Group
101	Stan Evenson Design, Inc.
109	The Graphics Studio
117	April Greiman, Inc.
125	Hard Werken
133	Wayne Hunt Design, Inc.
141	Looking/John Clark
149	Louey/Rubino Design Group
157	Maddocks & Company
165	Norman Moore/Design Art, Inc.
173	Ph.D
181	Sargent & Berman
189	Shiffman Young Design
197	Shimokochi/Reeves Design
205	Siegel & Gale/Cross
213	Patrick Soo Hoo Designers
221	SoS: Los Angeles
229	Sussman/Prejza & Co, Inc.
237	Vrontikis Design Office
245	The Warren Group
253	White Design
261	Index

PREFACE

Five years ago, I edited a similar book on Los Angeles graphic design. The studios, even the newer ones, seemed immutable, and the well established studios seemed as if they would endure forever. In looking over that list and comparing it to the current one, I see some major changes. Some well established studios no longer exist, or have been sold or merged. Some well known designers have ceased studio operations to function as consultants.

In comparing the lists I see a hundred percent increase in women principals and a more international attitude, with studio owners who were born and educated outside the United States.

The studios are all over the Los Angeles map and they are equally well distributed between the corporate and the playful, from fine art imagery to computerese.

The most obvious change in the work of the studios is the all-pervasive influence of the computer. In an amazingly short period, the computer has changed the way we work. Just as markers replaced chalks, the computer has changed the face of graphic design. Every studio in the book uses the computer-- some only use the computer.

The work remains varied--no Los Angeles look has emerged, or is it likely to. Though the business climate in this state has changed, and budgets and projects have become more restrictive, Los Angeles graphic design is still inventive, unexpected and bold-- just like Los Angeles.

Gerry Rosentswieg

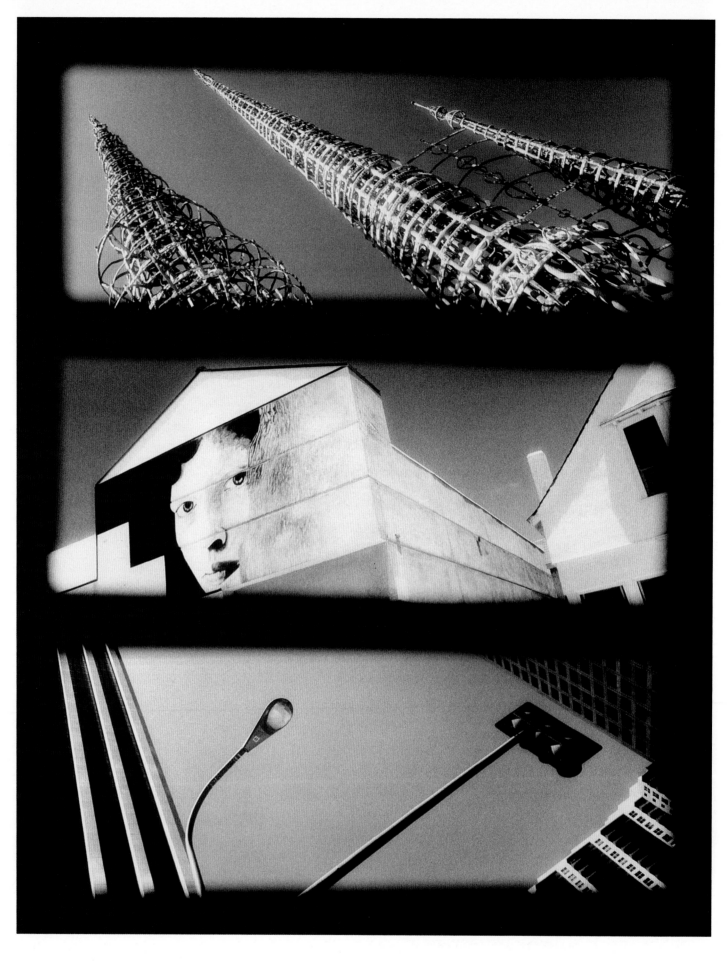

INTRODUCTION

As a native of Los Angeles, it's fascinating to see how much the city has changed. As a graphic designer for over thirty years, it's equally fascinating to see just how much our business has changed.

It's amazing how the two relate. In the 1950's, Los Angeles was manageable--it was within grasp. This was a community— where it was possible to know your neighbors, and with a little effort, you could know most of your peers—the other Los Angeles graphic designers.

There was an energy and a camaraderie in our profession, only partly prompted by the size of the community. There were design breakthroughs happening here and everyone knew it. The annual report as we know it today, was created in Los Angeles. The record industry allowed illustrators, photographers and graphic designers the freedom to experiment, which led to innovative styles which became the signatures of the sixties and seventies. And the film industry, in an effort to compete with television, created the art of movie titles.

One reason we had this freedom was geography. We were in Los Angeles, thousands of miles from the traditional centers of business. In the East, the business of graphic design was much more serious, just as business was more serious. There, the financial and corporate worlds kept a firm hold on the reins. Here, we were inventing businesses, lifestyles, and graphic design.

Organizations like the Association of Graphic Design (AGD) and the Art Directors Club of Los Angeles (ADLA) were formal ways to meet with each other. But the informal evenings in design studios—playing pool, drinking beer and talking design—were probably more valuable.

The ADLA meetings were a great source of inspiration and energy. They were held at The Masquer's Club. There would be a cocktail hour where you could go from table to table, talking to designers who became your comrades. Then there would be dinner, followed by a designer's presentation of his work. Everyone looked forward to those meetings.

And then there was Aspen. The Aspen Design Conference was one of the most important connections we had with designers from the rest of the country and the world. There, we could meet and share ideas not only with each other but with members of related fields—architects, industrial and interior designers, as well as sociologists, psychiatrists and philosophers who all had their own theories of how design fit into our world.

As a community of graphic designers, we've grown not only in numbers over the past thirty years, but in sophistication and ability. Just as the tools have changed from chalk comps to computer comps, the universities and professional schools have changed from afterthoughts of the fine art department to slick organizations cranking out new professionals.

All in all, we've kept pace with the city, moving in many directions, matching the diversity of Los Angeles with many styles and attitudes of graphic design. And yet, we've also stayed the same. After all, we're still inventing this business.

Jim Cross

KIMBERLY BAER DESIGN ASSOCIATES

KIMBERLY BAER DESIGN ASSOCIATES

When Kimberly Baer was a student at the University of California at Santa Cruz, she trained as a printmaker. After finishing school, Baer moved to Los Angeles and found that her real passion was design. "I loved design," she says. "Even as a fine artist I was always very interested in type."

Baer relocated to New York, where she joined Corporate Annual Reports, Inc., and spent two years working on annual reports. It was in New York that she met designer Barbara Cooper, now an invaluable member of her team. "We're really more like partners," Baer explains.

Returning to California in 1982, she opened Kimberly Baer Design Associates, located first in Pasadena, then in Venice. The firm handles brochures, annual reports, and identity programs for a list of clients ranging from restaurants to high tech.

More and more, the designers are working straight through to film on their computers, which Baer finds slightly ironic. "Everyone here comes from a tradition of doing letterpress books," she explains. "And here we are working on Photoshop."

1

2

3

5

4

6

1. Studio interior.
2. Annual report for The Gas Company.
3. Direct mail promotion for Hunt-Wesson, Inc highlighting its product's health benefits.
4. Annual report for the Santa Monica Bay Restoration Project.
5. Quarterly magazine for UCLA.
6. Annual report for a waste management company.

1

2

3

4

KIMBERLY BAER DESIGN ASSOCIATES

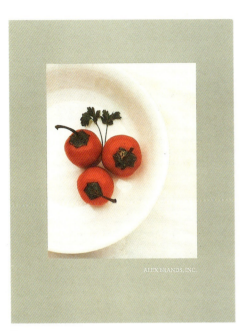

5

6

7

1. Annual report for a manufacturer of fiber optic testing equipment.
2. Symbol for an Italian restaurant.
3. Symbol for a restaurant.
4. Logo for a cafe.
5.-6. Capability brochure for a food manufacturer.
7. Leasing brochure.

KIMBERLY BAER DESIGN ASSOCIATES

1

2

3

4

5

StarBase

6

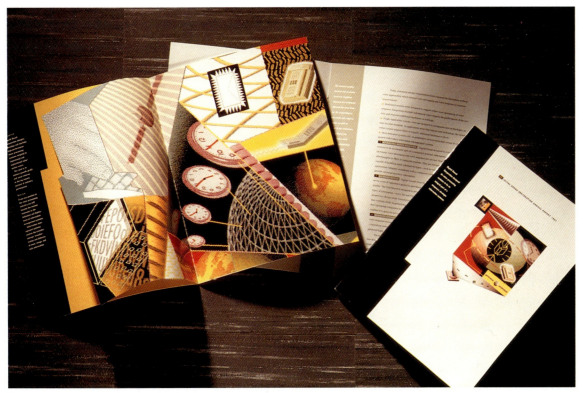

7

1.-2. Annual report for the California Lottery.

3. Annual report for the Los Angeles YMCA.

4. Symbol for The John E. Anderson Graduate School of Management at UCLA.

5. Symbol for a software company.

6. Symbol for a "street music" recording label.

7.-8. Annual and quarterly reports for Digital Sound, Inc. a manufacturer of voice mail equipment.

8

KIMBERLY BAER DESIGN ASSOCIATES

620 Hampton Drive   Venice, CA 90291   310.399.3295   fax 310.399.7964

1

2

1. Annual report for a manufacturer of connective devices for computers.
2. Capability brochure for a real estate firm.
3. Annual report for a manufacturer of recreational and industrial products.

3

BAKER DESIGN ASSOCIATES

BAKER DESIGN ASSOCIATES

"I think you can give good creative and good service, too", says Gary Baker, principal of Baker Design Associates. "I try to push the creative edge, but I also realize I'm in the service business."

His Santa Monica firm delivers mostly corporate design, including annual reports, capability brochures, sales and marketing tools, product and service brochures and identity programs.

Baker, who attended Art Center College of Design and graduated from UCLA, started his company in 1984. As his business has grown, he's found his duties changing. "I had to make the transition from being a designer and conceptualizing to managing, acting more as creative director." He continues, "Clients are looking for extended value for what they're spending."

He believes that great creative comes from a great environment in which to work. "I like to keep a positive environment, and keep people happy," he explains. "We have a team approach here. People talk to each other."

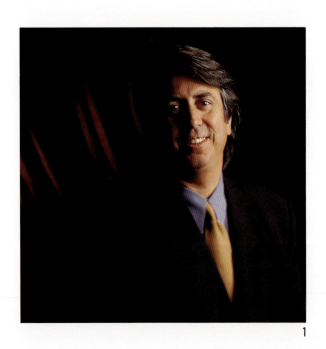

1

B d a

1. Gary Baker.
2. Retail store exterior.
3. Promotional shopping bag.
4. Logo for a clothing store.

2

3

Bernini

4

BAKER DESIGN ASSOCIATES

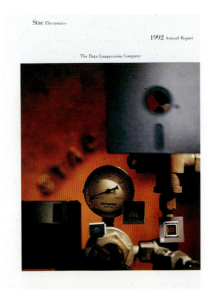

1

2

3

4

5

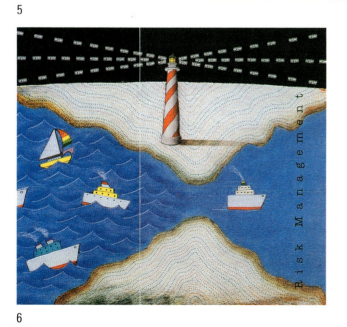
6

7

1.-2. Annual report.
3. Photo detail from above annual.
4.-5. Annual report for Southern California Physicians Insurance Exchange.
6.-7. Illustration details from above.

25

BAKER DESIGN ASSOCIATES

1.-2. Fundraising materials for the Los Angeles Music Center.
3. Logo for a software company.
4. Symbol for AIDS research awareness.
5. Logo for a company that produces 3D castings based on CAD designs.
6. Symbol for USC/Norris Comprehensive Cancer Center.
7.-8. Annual report for a company that manufactures personal care products.
9.-10. Annual report for a security company.
11.-12. University recruitment brochure.

logik^e

3

together for the cure

4

3D SYSTEMS INC

5

NORRIS

6

7

8

9

10

11

12

BAKER DESIGN ASSOCIATES

1450 20th Street   Santa Monica, CA 90404   310.453.6613   fax 310.453.4015

1.- 2. Race track annual report.
3. Detail of illustration from above report.

BASS YAGER & ASSOCIATES

BASS YAGER & ASSOCIATES

1

Bass Yager is an international design and marketing firm that was founded by design pioneer, Saul Bass. Graphic design is at the firm's core, with special emphasis on corporate identification programs, packaging, retail architecture and film.

The company has serviced some clients since their initial contact. "AT & T has been a client for 25 years," says Tony Asher, Bass Yager president. "We've had to learn so much about what they're doing, they consider us a part of their brain trust."

In 1978, the firm initiated its retail architecture department by creating a worldwide, unified marketing image for the Exxon Corporation. Included in the Exxon/Esso re-image were graphic systems, signage systems, packaging, uniforms, and vehicles, as well as architecture. Exxon has remained with the firm for the last 15 years.

"One reason for our longevity and success is that we tell clients the truth even when it's not to our advantage," Asher explains. "It's funny that our clients hire us as a design firm, because what they really get is more. They get our thinking."

2

6

1. Herb Yager, Saul Bass and Tony Asher.
2.-9. Identity programs created by the studio.
3. Symbol for KIA Motors.
8. Gas station design.

3

7

4

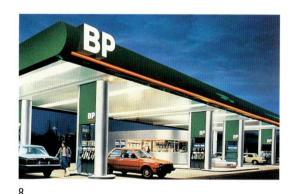
8

5

9

BASS YAGER & ASSOCIATES

1

1. Identity for a Japanese cosmetic company.
2. Symbol for a Japanese construction company.
3.-4. Identity and signage for a Japanese sporting goods manufacturer.
5. Identity for Maglite.

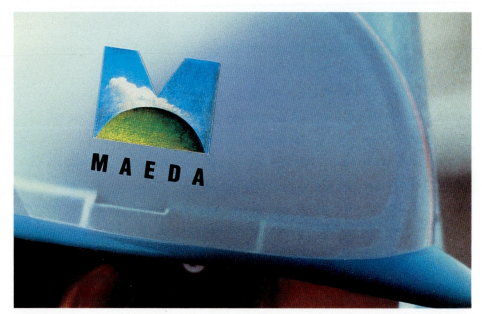

2

33

3

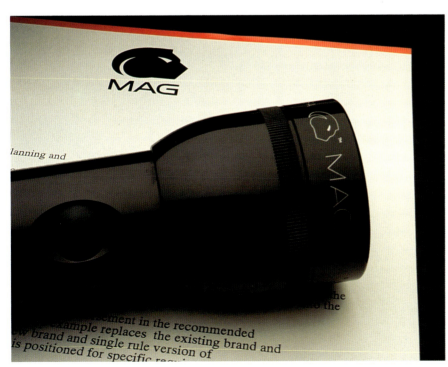
5

4

BASS YAGER & ASSOCIATES

34

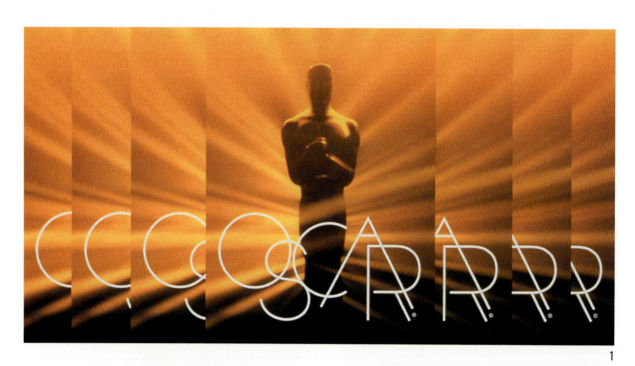

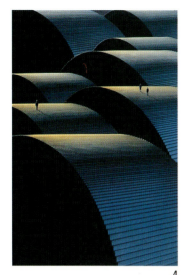

4

1. Poster for the Academy Awards.
2. Poster commemorating the Bicentennial of Human Rights.
3. Catalog cover.
4-5. Poster and book cover.

5

BASS YAGER & ASSOCIATES

7039 W. Sunset Boulevard   Los Angeles, CA 90038   213.466.9701   fax 213.466.9700

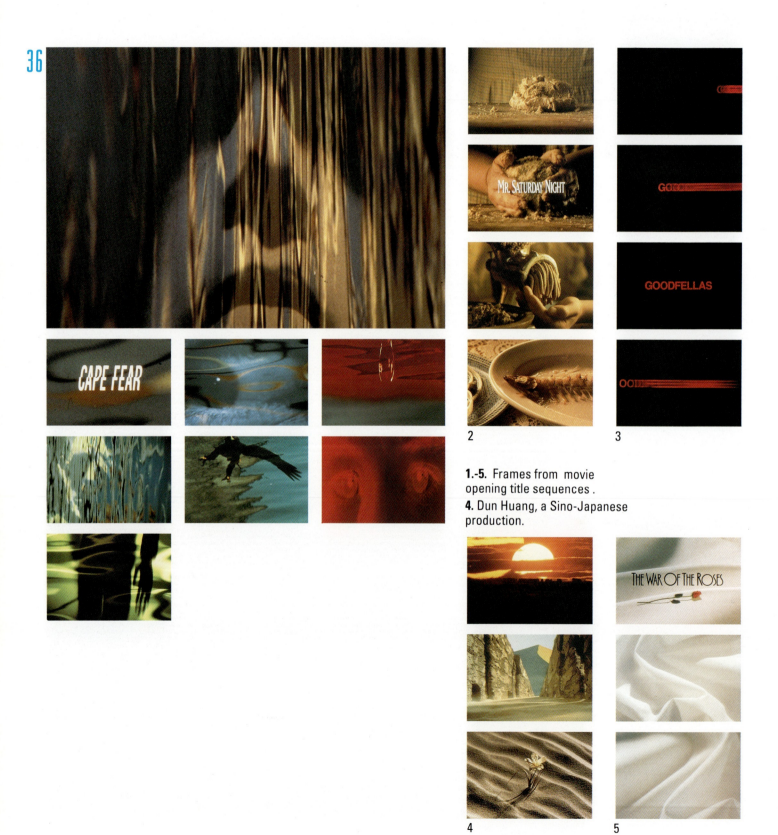

1.-5. Frames from movie opening title sequences.
4. Dun Huang, a Sino-Japanese production.

BESSER JOSEPH PARTNERS

BESSER JOSEPH PARTNERS

Rik Besser and Doug Joseph met fifteen years ago while attending the Art Center College of Design. After working as senior designers for six years, they founded their design firm in 1986. "We've been around each other for so long it's scary at times how much we think alike," Joseph says.

The firm, which develops marketing communications, packaging, and annual reports, services clients in diverse industries, including consumer products, entertainment, financial services, food and technology.

"We split almost everything down the middle," Joseph explains. "We both design and we both have administrative responsibilities. The office operates as a group, our clients are familiar with Rik and I as well as the rest of our staff."

The firm has won numerous awards, and their work has appeared in such publications as Communication Arts, Graphis, Idea, Industrial Design, Print and The Wall Street Journal.

1

2

1.-2. Office interior.
3.-4. Promotion and swatchbooks for Hopper Papers.

BESSER JOSEPH PARTNERS

1

2

3

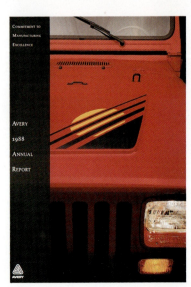

5

6

1.-2. Annual report for Unocal Corporation.
3.-4. Annual report for a personal products manufacturer.
5.-6. Annual report for Avery.
7.-8. Annual report for Lincoln Bancorp.
9.-10. Annual report for Agouron Pharmaceuticals.
11.-12. Annual report for Lockheed Corporation.

7

8

9

10

11

12

BESSER JOSEPH PARTNERS

42

1

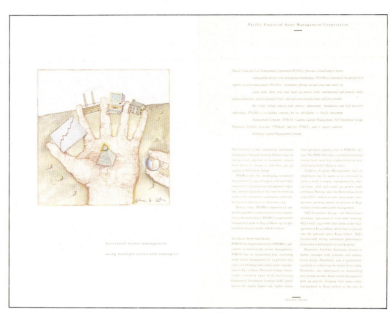
2

4

3

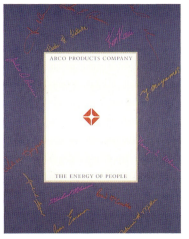
5

6

1.-2. Annual report for an insurance company.
3.-4. Capability brochure for a printer.
5.-6. Capability brochure for a division of Arco.
7. Risk management manual for The Doctors Company.

7

BESSER JOSEPH PARTNERS

1546 7th Street   Santa Monica, CA 90401   310.458.1899   fax 310.394.1789

44

1

2

1.-2. Packaging for bakery products.

BRIGHT & ASSOCIATES

BRIGHT & ASSOCIATES

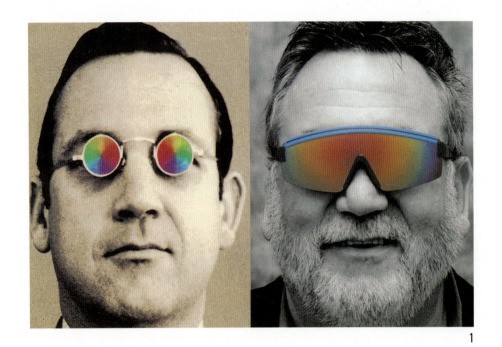

1

Housed in the former offices of Charles and Ray Eames, Venice-based Bright & Associates has earned hundreds of awards and international attention developing highly visible marks and design programs for clients such as Coca Cola, Thrifty Drugs, Ryder Trucks, Holland America and Western Digital, among others.

Although the firm develops identity programs, collateral systems, interior and exterior signage and environments and merchandising, the firm's emphasis has recently been on packaging systems. "Packaging is now our number one priority." principal Keith Bright explains.

Having been in the business for over thirty years, Bright has developed ten simple rules of design: 1. Make it big. 2. Keep it simple. 3. Does it feel good? 4. Work fast. 5. Design with clients' problems in mind. 6. Don't complain. 7. Use big type. 8. Don't use bastardized typography. 9. Have fun. and 10. Listen!,listen!, listen!.

2

3

4

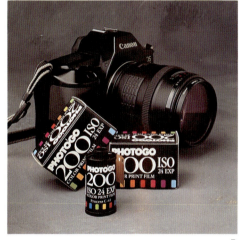

5

1. Promotional poster created for the 50th anniversary of the Art Director's Club of Los Angeles, *Keith Bright, Time Flies.*
2. Package design.
3. Symbol and tag for Taiwan products.
4. Identity application for a casino.
5. Photo identity application.

BRIGHT & ASSOCIATES

48

1

2

3

4

1. Collateral materials for a golf and tennis equipment manufacturer.
2. Package design.
3. Package design for eyecare products.
4. "Taste It All" campaign tagline units.
5. Symbol for China External Trade Development Council.
6. Identity for a beauty salon.
7. Symbol for Pinkerton Security Systems.
8. Symbol for LA Sports Council.
9. Symbol for Roland Music.
10. Symbol for US Badminton Open Championship.
11. Symbol for Western Digital.
12. Symbol for CETRA.
13. Symbol for Resort at Squaw Creek.
14. Symbol for California/EPA.
15. Symbol for Visual Edge.
16. Symbol for Canadian Badminton Open Championship.

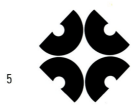

5

11

6

12

7

13

8

14

9

15

10

16

BRIGHT & ASSOCIATES

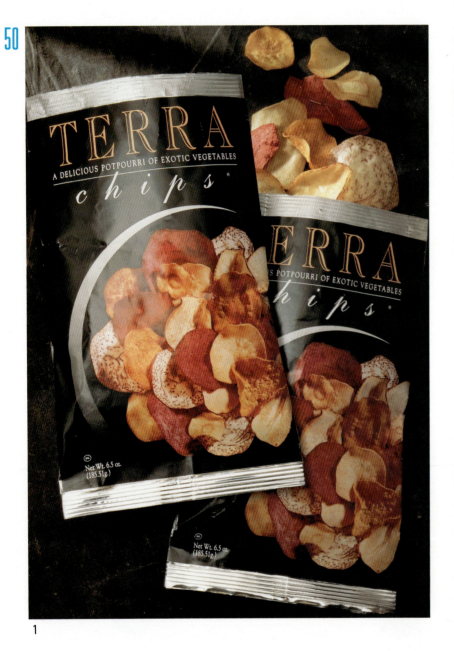

1

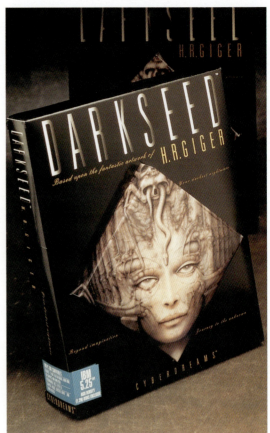

2

3

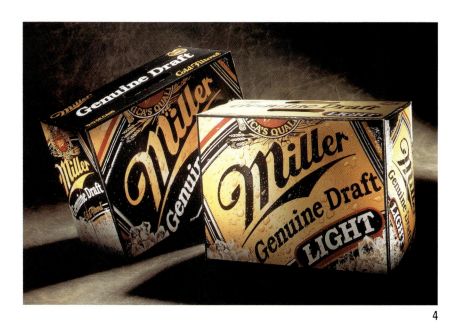

1. Package design for vegetable chips.
2. Package design for a computer game.
3. Identity for the Speedway Cafe.
4. Package design.
5. Food packaging.
6. Marauchi Furniture identity application.

BRIGHT & ASSOCIATES

901 Washington Boulevard   Venice, CA 90291   310.450.2488   fax 310.452.1613

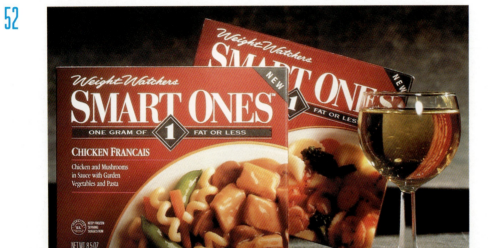

1

3

1. Package design.
2. Identity for retail car audio chain.
3. Airline identity for Aviatecha, the national airline of Guatemala.
4. Identity and package design.

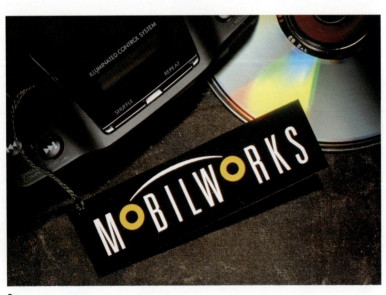

2

4

MICHAEL BROCK DESIGN

MICHAEL BROCK DESIGN

Steeped in a background of publication design, Michael Brock began his career at NASA, designing marketing presentations. From there, he was launched into editorial design, joining Meredith Publications and then Playboy Enterprises.

In 1981, Brock moved to California and opened his own design firm, where he continues to specialize in publication design, along with corporate and entertainment collateral. Until recently, Michael served as design director for L.A. Style, while maintaining his own design firm. Besides editorial design, he and his staff develop corporate identity, sales and marketing collateral, point-of-purchase and packaging.

Brock, who holds a Master of Fine Arts degree from the University of Alabama, services a diverse client list, such as Warner Home Video, RCA/Columbia, The Institute for Families of Blind Children, Time Inc. Magazine and MCA Records, among others. Michael was recently appointed to the United States Citizens Stamp Advisory Committee which meets quarterly to recommend stamp subjects and designs to the Postmaster General.

The designer's elegant style emanates from a disciplined approach. "For every problem, I can immediately come up with a solution that would work," he explains. "But then I put it aside and try to develop a more unique approach."

1

2

3

4

5

6

7

1. Michael Brock.
2. L.A. Style media kit.
3. Real estate brochure.
4. Advertisement for 360 Systems.
5. Resort brochure.
6. Anniversary poster.
7. Capabilities brochure for a printer.

MICHAEL BROCK DESIGN

56

1

4

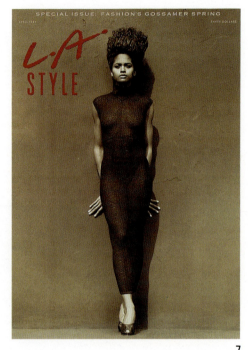

7

2

5

1. Symbol for a recording studio.
2. Identity for a restaurant.
3. Identity for an antique dealer.
4. Symbol for a high-tech manufacturer.
5. Icon for a magazine department.
6. Symbol for a film syndication company.
7.-12. Magazine covers.
13. Advertising supplement for Chrysler.

3

6

57

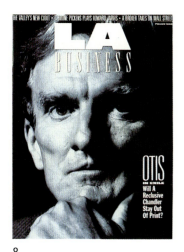

8

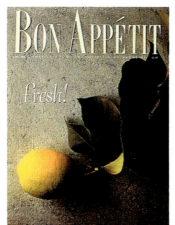

10

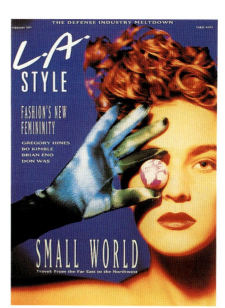

12

9

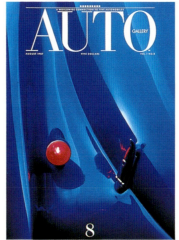

11

13

MICHAEL BROCK DESIGN

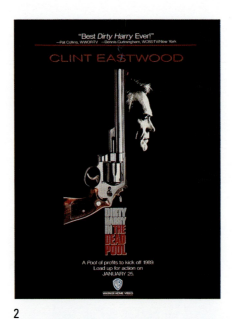

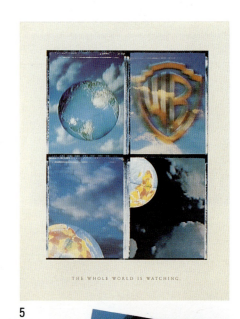

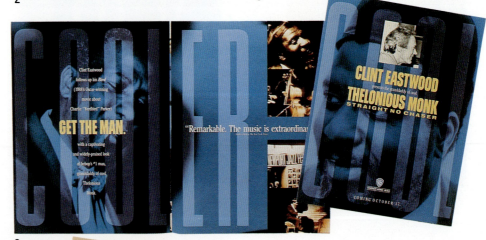

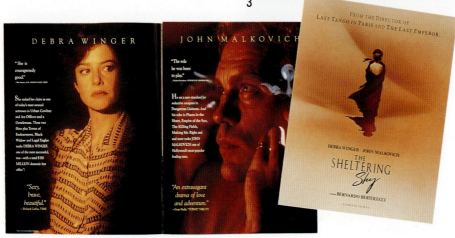

1. Point-of-purchase standee.
2. Movie collateral material.
3. Video collateral material
4. Movie promotional material.
5. Advertising insert.
6.-7. Home video catalog.
8.-9. Video packaging.
10. Home video catalog.

6

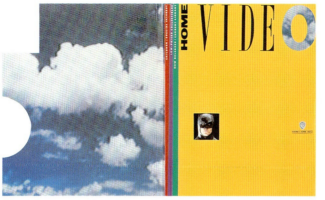

7

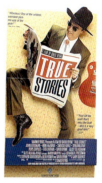

8

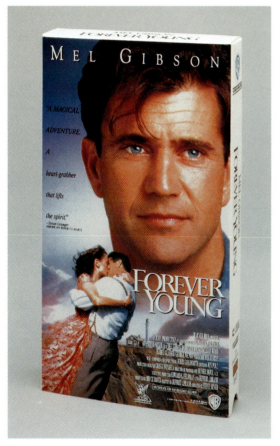

9

10

MICHAEL BROCK DESIGN

8075 W. 3rd Street #300   Los Angeles, CA 90048   213.932.0283   fax 213.932.8165

60

1

2

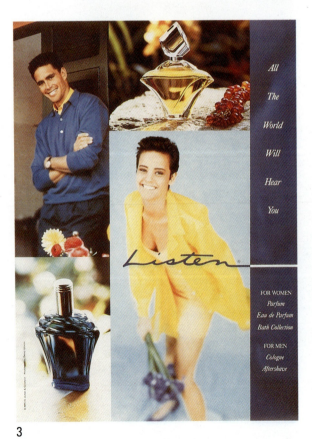

3

4

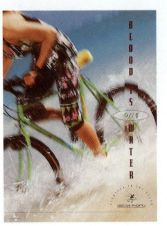

5

1.-2. Package designs for a food condiment company.
3. Advertisement for a perfume.
4. Promotional desk calendar for L.A. Style Magazine.
5. Advertisement for sportswear.

MARGO CHASE DESIGN

When asked to speak at colleges and seminars, designer Margo Chase often brings along a slide show she created, called "Germs". In it, she shows finished product juxtaposed with its inspiration. A curve in a wrought iron fence might become a type treatment, for instance. "People always ask me how I get my ideas, so I thought I should show some sources," she explains.

But the name of her show bespeaks more than her mode of idea generation. It also reflects her past, which is one of science and medicine. In fact, for most of her pre-design life she was convinced she would become a veterinarian. And in school, at the University of California at San Francisco, she was working toward her masters in medical illustration, when she defected to Los Angeles to become a designer. Her reason was simple: "The design students were more interesting. They dressed weird and had very cool hair."

After several years of freelancing Chase opened her own studio in 1986. Situated on the side of a hill in the Silverlake district, her multi-level, two-story, glass and wood house contains floor-to-ceiling bookcases, collected artifacts and various pieces, like the Dracula monster/gargoyle sculpture she designed for the Francis Ford Coppola movie campaign.

Chase's projects skew heavily toward music and entertainment, with clients such as Warner Records, Geffen Records, Atlantic Records, Radio Vision, Virgin Records and Harmony Pictures. She creates logos, identity programs, CD covers and packaging that express her unique background.

She explains, "I get a lot of satisfaction out of working in the music industry because it allows me the freedom to create unusual imagery."

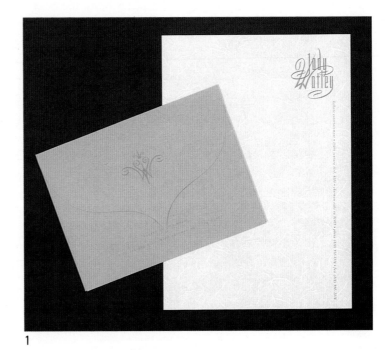

1

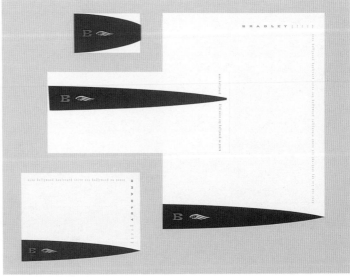

2

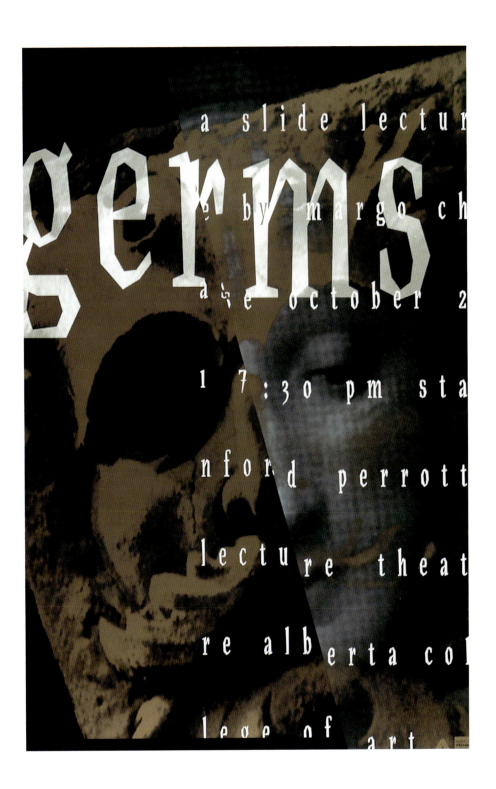

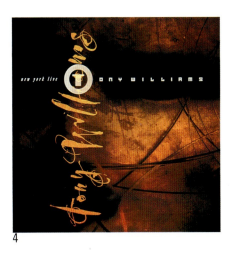
4

5

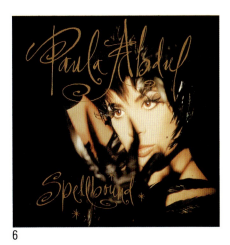
6

1. Personal stationery.
2. Stationery system for a computer dealer who specializes in graphics workstations.
3. Poster designed to announce a lecture given by Margo Chase.
4. Video disc packaging.
5-6. CD package designs.

MARGO CHASE DESIGN

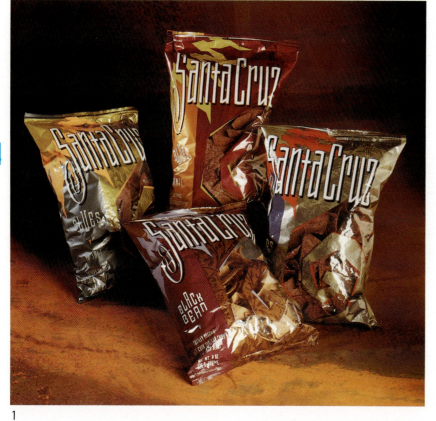
1

2

3

4

1. Package design for gourmet chip line.
2-3. CD cover designs.
4. Generic record sleeve for Virgin Records.
5. Logo design for a CD promotion.
6. CD package design.
7. Logo design for a band, used on CD covers and promotional materials.
8.-9. Promotional poster and packaging for haircare products.

5

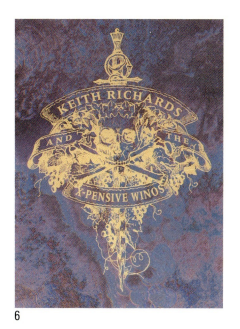
6

7

8

9

1

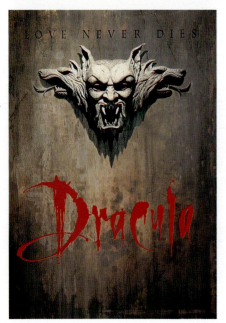

2

3

4

5

6

M A R G O   C H A S E   D E S I G N

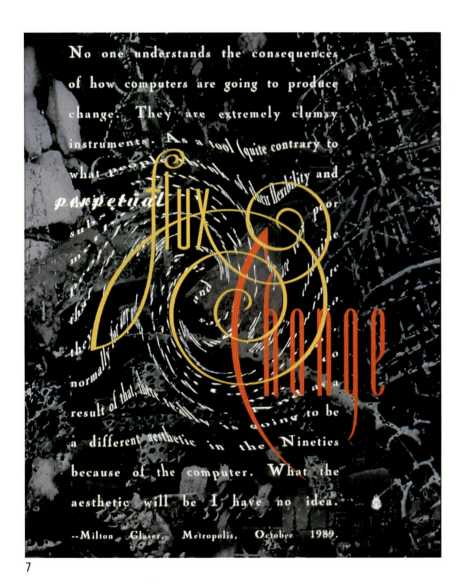

7

8

9

10

1.-2. Posters created as teasers for a feature motion picture.
3.-6. Spreads from the architecture magazine Semiotext(e). 3.-4. is an interview with filmmaker, Atom Egoyan and 5.-6. is an article on the image of women in film.
7. Poster created for the Los Angeles Art Director's Club.
8.-9. Invitation for a department store fashion show.
10. Promotional wine labeling and packaging for a printer.

MARGO CHASE DESIGN

2255 Bancroft Avenue   Los Angeles, CA 90039   213.668.1055   fax 213.668.2470

1. Symbol for Radio Vision, a company that produces and markets concert films and videos.
2. Symbol for Sidney Cooper, photographer.
3. Logo for Yoyo, a rap musican.
4. Symbol and logo for an artist's representative.
5. Promotional logo for Capitol Records.

1

3

2

4

5

COY, LOS ANGELES

COY, LOS ANGELES

From packaging to collateral to advertising, a Coy, Los Angeles, project is usually playful, witty and full of style. Founded in 1978, the firm attracts clients who are willing to step away from the conventional.

"We work with arts organizations, contract designers, interior designers, architects and film companies," explains Margaret Coy, executive director. "We have a pretty varied list." Besides corporate work, the firm develops posters, barricades, signage and promotional systems.

John Coy, creative director, has been designing since 1969. He oversees the creative process while Margaret handles administrative duties. "We share the marketing aspects," she says.

1. Identity for the studio.
2. Capability brochure for an architectural firm.
3. Packaging and promotion for a winery.
4. Sculpture created for a paper company's recycled paper promotion.

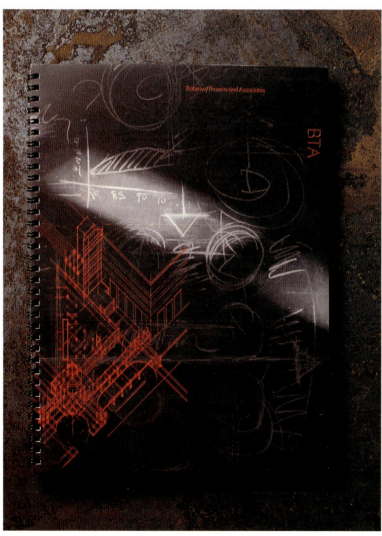

2

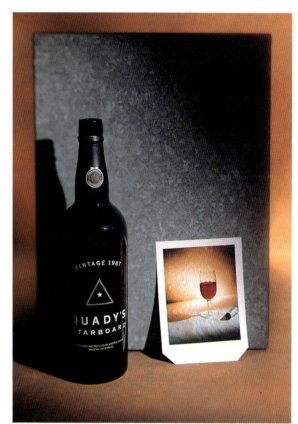

3

4

COY, LOS ANGELES

1

2

3

1. Capital campaign materials for the Newport Harbor Art Museum.
2. Aids awareness poster.
3. Advertising photography for a furniture manufacturer.
4. Advertising photography for a textile manufacturer.
5. Page from a calendar featuring celebrity caricatures by American designers. The celebrity featured is fine artist Jonathan Borofsky.

4

5

COY, LOS ANGELES

1. Packaging for a men's cosmetic line.
2. Symbol for a film production company.
3. Logo for a transprtation line.
4. Identity for a product line.
5. Symbol for a restaurant.
6. Symbol for a museum.
7. Logo for an opera production.
8. Logo for the Riordan Foundation.
9. Logo for a museum fundraising event featuring decorative tablewaare.
10. Symbol for a Japanese restaurant.

2

5

8

3

6

9

VITAMIN SOURCE

4

The Marriage of Figaro
MOZART

7

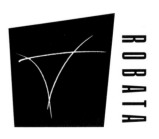

10

COY, LOS ANGELES

9520 Jefferson Boulevard   Culver City, CA 90232   310.837.0173   fax 310.559.1706

1

2

1. Signage program.
2. Retail center advertising campaign.

CURRY DESIGN

Curry Design

From the conservative to the playful, Curry Design develops a broad variety of projects for a diverse group of clients. "We don't specialize," explains principal Steve Curry. "We're generalists. We do a little of everything. We might do an annual report, packaging, or a project like baseball cards for Upper Deck."

Steve, who was raised in Northern California and graduated from Long Beach State in 1982, founded his company in 1988. Before that, he worked at several design firms, including Bright & Associates, Douglas Boyd Design & Marketing and Rusty Kay & Associates.

Curry enjoys the diversity of his client list. "Everyone is different," he says. "One client might have his TV blaring and his dog barking while you're trying to present a campaign for the whole year. Or you might run the gauntlet of an entire marketing department, refining and re-refining a project until they feel it is ready to show the CEO. The end result is the same, we're trying to show and produce good work."

1

2

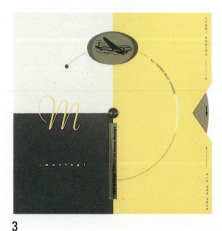

3

4

5

7

6

1. Curry Design staff. l. to r. Chona Bagsik, Jason Scheideman, Steve Curry and Kris Tibor.

2. Promotional mailing of packaged sweatshirts with the company logo.

3. Moving announcement for Curry Design.

4. Holiday packaging for a typographer.

5. Holiday packaging.

6. Automotive speakers packaging, targeted to young consumers.

7. Promotional wine package for a typographer.

CURRY DESIGN

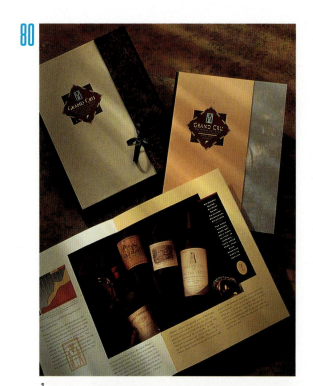

1

3

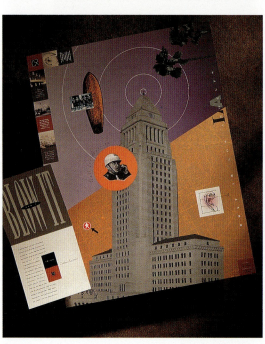

2

4

5

1. Brochure for a fine wine investment opportunity.
2. Call for entries poster/mailer for the Los Angeles Art Director's Club.
3. Annual and quarterly reports for L.A. Gear.
4. Page from a promotional calendar for a printer and a paper company.
5. Labeling for Heritage Beer Co.
6. Self-promotion holiday packaging.

6

CURRY DESIGN

1

2

3

4

5

6

7

8

9

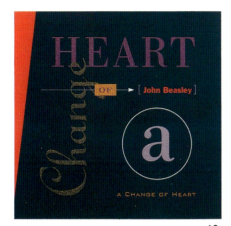

10

1. Symbol for Imagine Films.
2. Symbol for Grand Cru Fund, a wine investment firm.
3. Logo for a typographer.
4. Logo for a unique gift store.
5. Symbol for a mortgage broker, Pacific Lending Group.
6. Symbol for Aroma Vera, an aroma therapy and skin care company.
7. Symbol for women's junior swimwear.
8. Logo for Western Typography Associates.
9. Symbol for Skilset Typographers.
10. CD packaging.
11. Promotional delivery labels for a typographer.

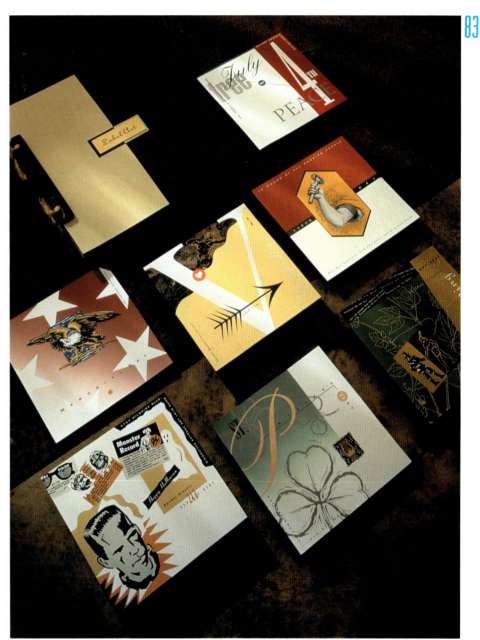

11

CURRY DESIGN

1501 Main Street   Venice CA 90291   310.399.4626   fax 310.399.8524

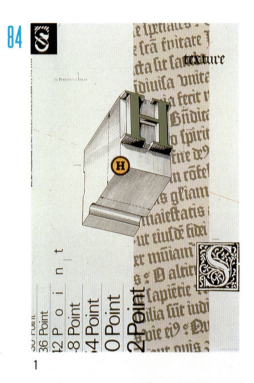

1

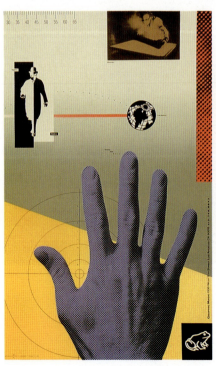

2

3

4

1. Promotional poster for a typographer.
2. Poster for a quality silk screen printer.
3. Annual report for IDB Communications.
4. Packaging for a compact disk storage system.

THE DESIGNORY INC.

THE DESIGNORY INC.

Driven by car accounts, The Designory prides itself on being more a communications firm than simply a design service. To produce the range of work that they do, which includes brochures, point of sale materials and other marketing tools, The Designory works closely with their clients and their clients' advertising agencies. This type of partnership philosophy assures their clients that all marketing communications share the voice, image and objectives of the clients overall marketing program.

With a 14,000-square foot office and over 25 state-of-the art computer design stations, the Designory is not what you would call small. In fact, the Long Beach-based firm boasts an employee list of about 60 people--designers, art directors, writers, account executives, administrative support staff and more.

Over the last few years, the firm has done an extensive amount of work for companies based in the Pacific Rim, Europe and Canada. Dave Almquist, president, says, "What's helped us during our growth is great graphic design, solid account management and, first and foremost, intelligent. creative and effective communication design." Dave continues, "Design that doesn't make a contribution to the marketing objective of your client is only decorated paper and is a waste of time and money"

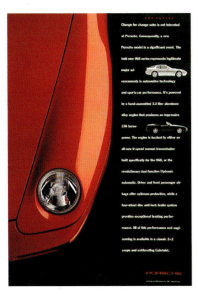

2

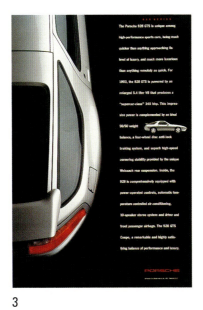

3

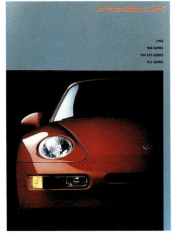

4

5

6

1. The Designory Staff.
2.-3. Dealer showroom posters for Porsche Cars North America.
4.-6. Brochure for Porsche.

1

2

3

4

THE DESIGNORY INC.

1.-4. Consumer brochure for Nissan Motor Corporation, USA.
5.-9. Brochure series for Nissan.

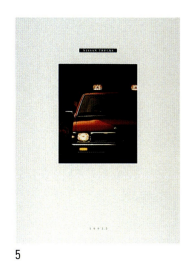
5

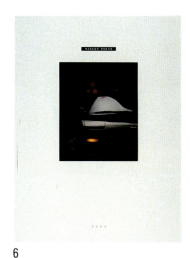
6

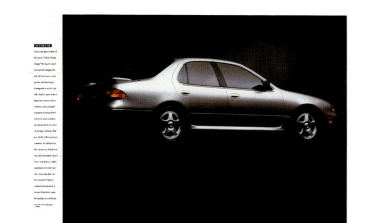
7

8

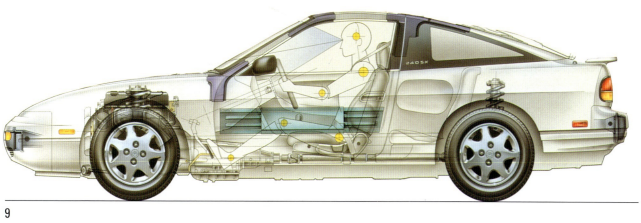
9

THE DESIGNORY INC.

90

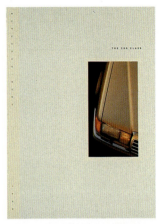
1

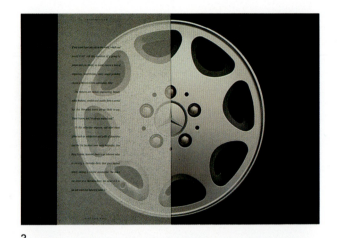
3

2

4

5

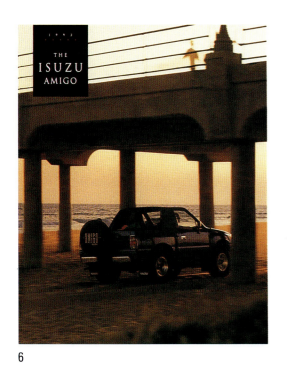
6

1.-5. Brochure series for Mercedes-Benz of North America, Inc.
6.-9. Consumer brochure series for American Isuzu Motors, Inc.

7

8

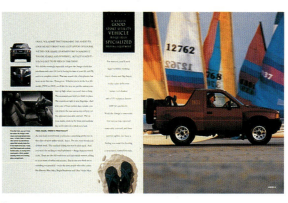
9

THE DESIGNORY INC.

211 E. Ocean Boulevard   Long Beach, CA 90802   310.432.5707   fax 310.491.0140

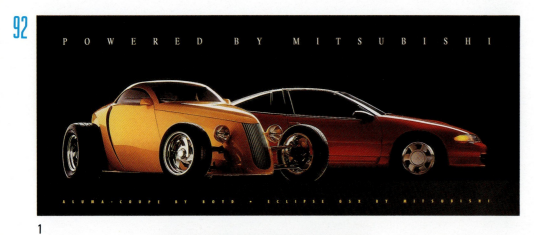

1

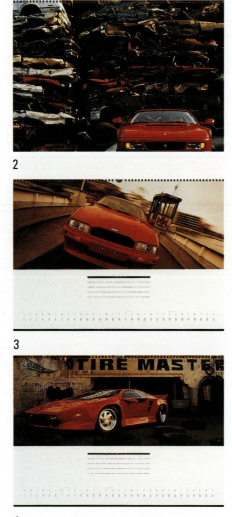

2

3

4

5

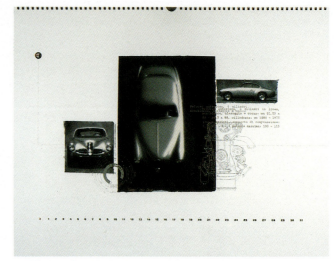

6

1. Poster for Mitsubishi Motor Sales of America, Inc.
2.-4. Promotional calendar for Road & Track magazine.
5.-6. Calendar for Alfa Romeo.

ROD DYER GROUP

ROD DYER GROUP

Rod Dyer had always wanted to design his own books. So he did. He always wanted to own a restaurant. So he does. And, he's always wanted to direct a movie. So now, he's going to.

A native of Johannesburg, South Africa, the award-winning designer is fueled by risk and inspiration. His staff, which hovers at around 25, includes designers from around the globe whose portfoilios may not have necessarily gotten them jobs elsewhere in town. "Their work is a little avant-garde. I like to hire people who are not run of the mill," Dyer says. "I guide them, but give them creative freedom, as well. They're talented, intelligent, and they get a grasp very quickly."

Dyer, whose design career spans 30 years, services mostly entertainment clients, including major film studios and cable and network television. 25% of the firm's work is in corporate design, developing advertising and annual reports. One corporate client, Jones Intercable has been working with Dyer for twenty years.

Lately, Dyer has found his biggest challenge is to develop design solutions in a more fiscally-responsible manner, given today's economic climate. "We've had to step back and say, we have to deliver the same quality of work for less money," he explains. "We now find ourselves spending more strategic time in problem solving. Before proceeding to a presentation stage, we resolve at pencil stage, refine two or three concepts and complete the project. I actually like it better. The results are more rewarding."

Dyer's personal goal for his clients is to give them design with longevity and panache.

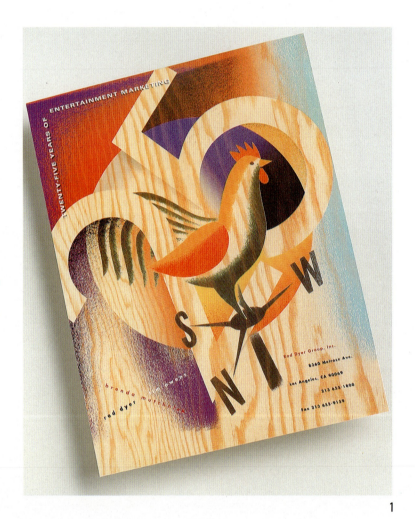

1

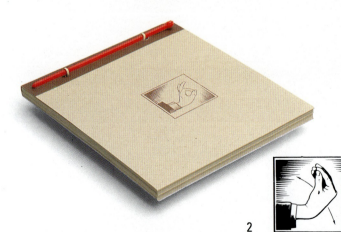

2

COSA VUOI? *FINITO* *INSISTO*
WHAT DO YOU FINISHED I INSIST
EXPECT

3

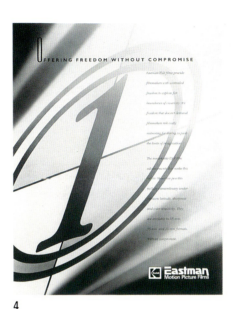

4

1. 25th anniversary announcement for the studio.
2. Promotional book for Dyer's restaurant, Pane e Vino, cataloging Italian hand signs.
3.-4. Advertising campaign for motion picture film.
5.-7. Brochure for the introduction of a new sound system for film.

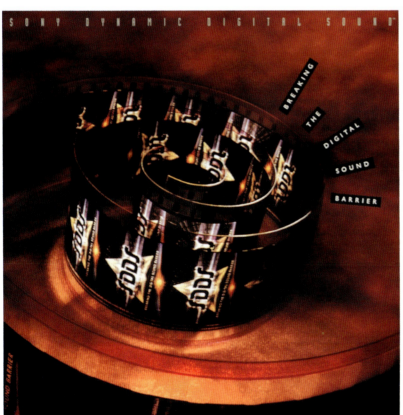

5

6

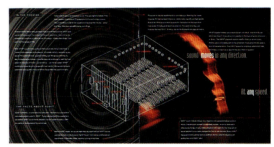

7

ROD DYER GROUP

1

2

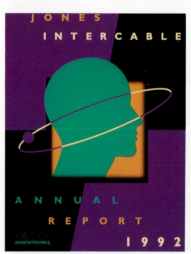
3

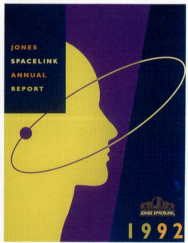
4

5

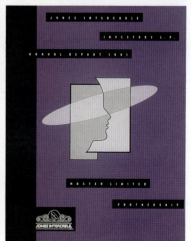
6

8. Symbol for a film distribution company.
9. Symbol for a film production company.
10. Rod Dyer Group Illustration.
11. Logo for an entertainment company.
12. Logo for a restaurant.
13. Personal mark.
14. Symbol for a film production company.

7

11

8

DRAGO

12

9

13

10

14

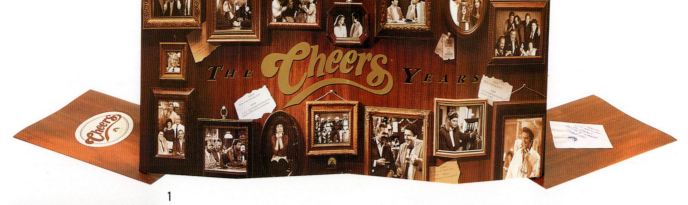

1

2   3   4

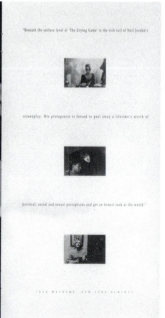

5

ROD DYER GROUP

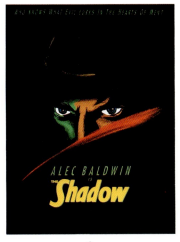
6

7

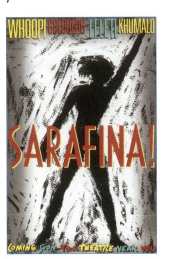
8

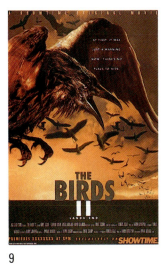
9

10

11

12

1. Magazine insert for the final episode of a popular television series.
2.-5. Brochure to bring a feature film to the attention of the Academy Award voters.
6.-8 Motion picture posters.
9. Keyart for a Made-for-Cable movie.
10.-11. Motion picture posters.
12. Film promotion brochure.

ROD DYER GROUP

8360 Melrose Avenue   Los Angeles, CA 90069   213.655.1800   fax 213.655.9159

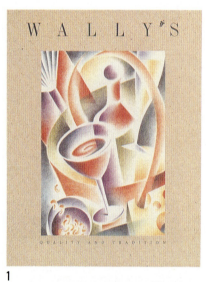

1

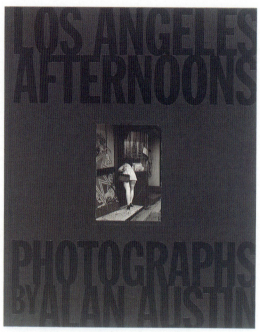

2

1. Mail order catalog for a wine merchant.
2. Book design.
3. T-shirt designs.

3

EVENSON DESIGN GROUP

EVENSON DESIGN GROUP

"Our clients range from extremely conservative to rock and roll," says Stan Evenson, principal and creative director of Evenson Design Group. His projects are equally diverse, ranging from fairly simple newsletters to intricate packaging to entire campaigns.

High on his list of prorities is pro-bono work. "I'm very dedicated to it," Evenson explains. "It's a civic duty that I really believe in. Whether times are tough, or not, it's important to fit it in." The firm has been very active with children's groups, such as the ERAS Center, an organization for children at risk, The American Child Foundation and California Literacy.

His staff numbers just under ten, five of whom are designers. Barbara Hamagami, who has been with the firm for fifteen years, serves as senior project director. "I have the designers act almost as account executives, dealing with the clients. It's a very good structure that has worked well for us."

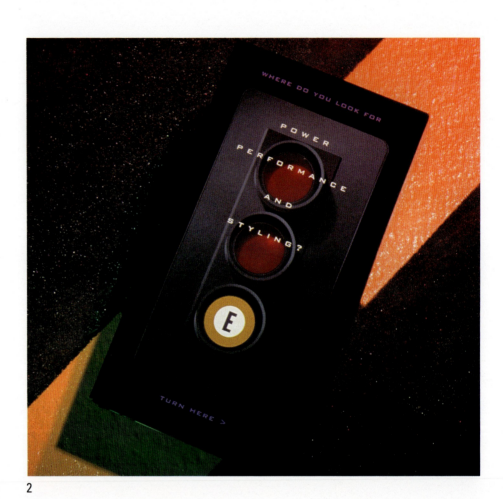

2

1

1. Stan Evenson.
2. The studio's self-promotional video.
3. Private Exercise exterior signage.
4. Stationery system for the private gym.
5. Bathroom door details.
6. Promotional clothing.

EVENSON DESIGN GROUP

1

2

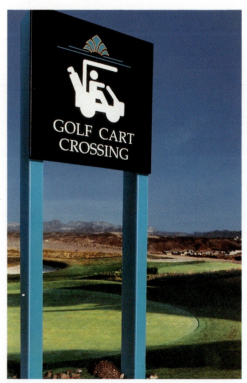

3

1. New England Patriots logo.
2. Marketing materials for a country club/resort.
3. Golf course signage.
4. CD and tape packaging.
5. Concert video packaging.
6.-7. CD packaging.

4

5

6

7

EVENSON DESIGN GROUP

1

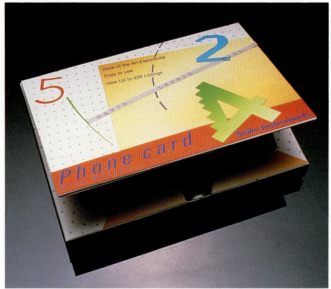

2

3

1. Promotional materials for a service bureau.
2. Packaging for an electronic phone card.
3. Pet food packaging.
4. Promotional binder for a service bureau.

4

1

5

9

2

6

10

3

7

11

4

8

1. Symbol for Clean-up Technology.
2. Proposed symbol for Private Exercise.
3. Symbol for Radio Gabby, a radio producer.
4. Symbol for BrooksHoward, a duplicating company.
5. Symbol for a health network of pet owners and veterinarians.
6. Symbol for a waterbed temperature control.
7. Proposed symbol for Apple's Learning Concepts Group.
8. Symbol for a school for children at risk.
9. Symbol for album to CD conversion.
10. Symbol for American Child Foundation.
11. Symbol for California Literacy.

E V E N S O N   D E S I G N   G R O U P

4445 Overland Avenue   Culver City, CA 90230   310.204.1995   fax 310.204.4879

108

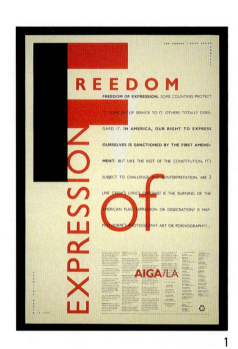

1

2

3

4

1. Freedom of Expression contest poster designed for AIGA/LA.
2. Holiday promotion.
3. U-Decorate-It Pinecone Kit, holiday self-promotion for the studio.
4. Reindeer Chips, a studio holiday promotion.

THE GRAPHICS STUDIO

THE GRAPHICS STUDIO

"I like to have fun with what I do," says Gerry Rosentswieg, principal of the The Graphics Studio. "And I like the fun to show!" With a client list that ranges from arts organizations to high-tech medical companies, for whom the studio develops everything from corporate identity to shopping bags, Rosentswieg's work might best be described as eclectic.

"For a small studio, we do a fair amount," the designer says. "That's what I like about this profession. New things are happening all the time--new projects and new clients and new things to learn."

The studio is filled with fine art that Rosentswieg has collected over the years. "I like California art," referring to a handsome, square metal painting by Billy Al Bengston, he comments, "That piece is simply light caught by folded metal. California art has always been about light," He continues, "I think fine art in the studio is necessary, these pieces are examples of creating without rules. An inspiration that frees the design process."

Six years ago, Rosentswieg began designing and editing books about graphic design. "I wanted to bring California design to national attention," he explains. His books include Graphic Design: Los Angeles, Graphic Design: San Francisco, The New Logo From California, and The New American Logo.

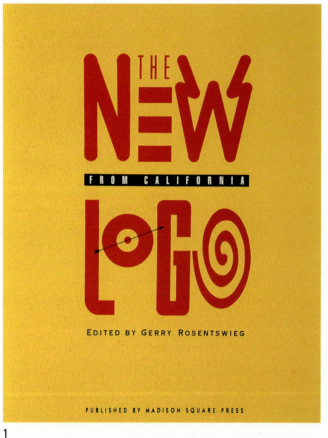

1

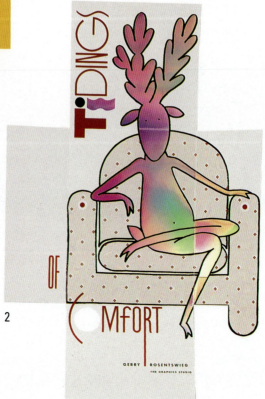

2

3

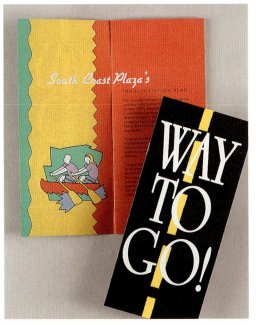

4

5

1. Book designed and edited by Gerry Rosentswieg.

2. Holiday greeting card for a printing foil manufacturer.

3. Capability brochure for an engineering management company.

4. Ridesharing brochure.

5. Poster and announcement mailer for an exhibit at The Japanese American Cultural Center.

THE GRAPHICS STUDIO

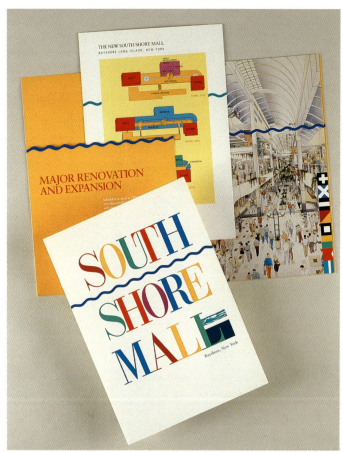

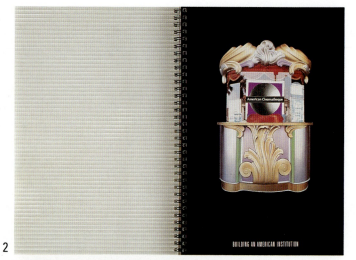

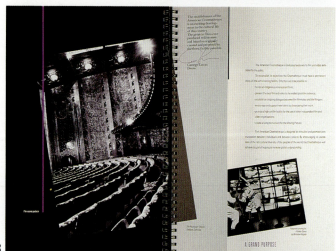

1. Leasing brochure for a shopping center.
2.-4. Fund raising brochure for American Cinematheque.
5.-6. Banners created to call attention to the regentrification of this art deco section of Wilshire Boulevard.
7. Book design.
8. Packaging for surgical corneal shields.

5

6

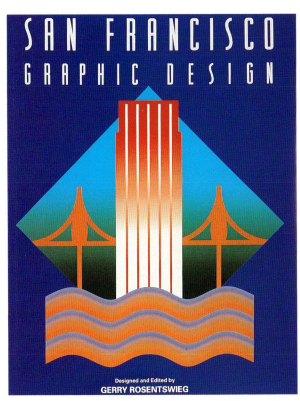

7

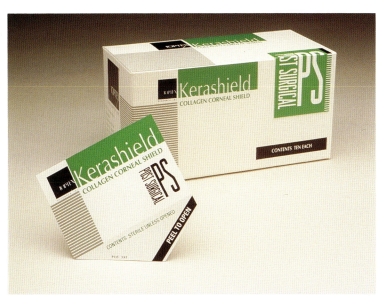

8

THE GRAPHICS STUDIO

114

1

2

3

4

5

6

7

8

9

10

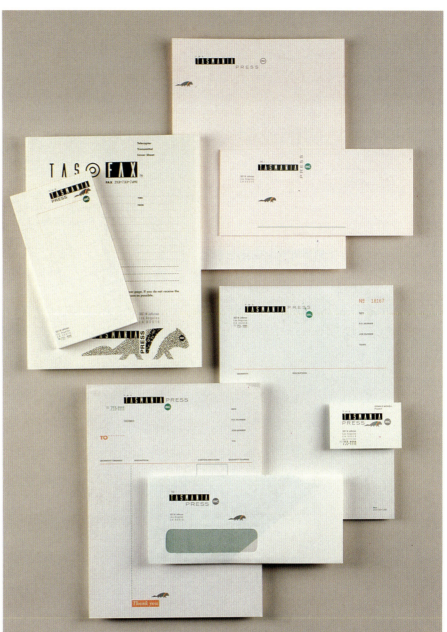
11

12

1. Storefront and lighting design for a funiture showroom.
2.-4. Shopping center leasing brochure.
5. Proposed symbol for Childrens Hospital.
6. Symbol for the Amie Karen Cancer Fund/LA Marathon fundraising promotion.
7. Symbol for Summer Communications, a public relations company.
8. Symbol for UCLA Film and Television Archives.
9. Symbol for a gym that has a gymnastic program.
10. Symbol for a real estate public service event
11. Stationery system for a printer
12. Promotional mini-poster for a printer.

THE GRAPHICS STUDIO

811 N. Highland Avenue   Los Angeles, CA 90038   213.466.2666   fax 213.466.5685

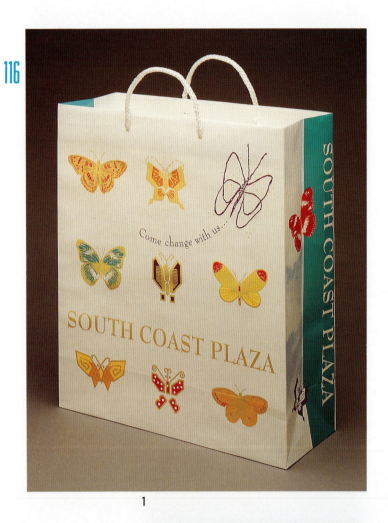

1

1. Promotional shopping bag for a shopping center.
2. Book/catalog design to accompany an exhibit sponsored by the Constitutional Rights Foundation.
3. Catalog design for a photography exhibit.
4. Book cover design for English as a second language textbooks.

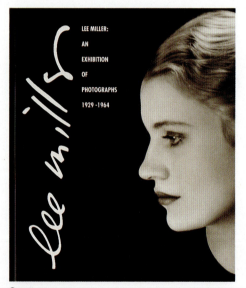

3

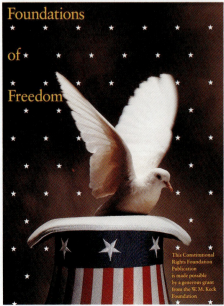

2

4

APRIL GREIMAN, INC.

APRIL GREIMAN, INC.

At the furthest end of her expansive warehouse loft, April Greiman sits. There, she talks on the phone. Confers with her staff. And designs. High above her, big blond pine frames containing April Greiman posters hang in a precise line, stretching from one end of the studio to the other, strung up with wire in what one designer calls, "the Grand Guillotine of Design".

The posters are multi-faceted, multi-media lessons on collage, type design and wit. Layer upon layer of words, images and color convey meanings and messages one may not be able to grasp in one glance.

"If the Basel school is the reduction method, ours would be the additive method," laughs Greiman. "I'm interested in putting in as much information as is appropriate."

Greiman, who, when asked how long she's been designing says, "Since birth!", has been designing professionally since 1972. She began attracting attention when she started importing video imagery into her print work. And now she designs video projects, as well.

Awarded the "Hall Chair" Fellowship by Hallmark in 1989, Greiman has served as Director of the Visual Communications department at California Institute of the Arts, and has been featured on numerous news shows on stations including CNN, PBS and ESPN.

Also awarded Most Improved Player by her softball league two summers in a row, Greiman says the firm's most interesting projects are, "the ones where I have no idea what I'm going to do. Almost everything we do has never been done before."

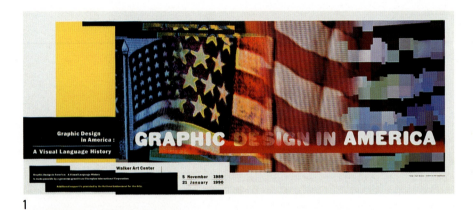
1

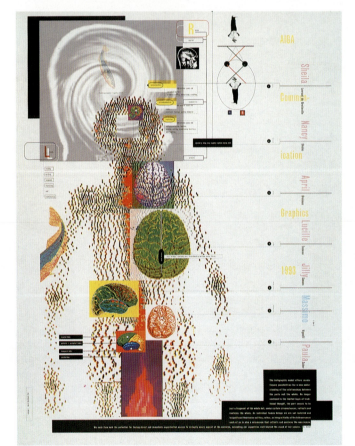
2

3

4

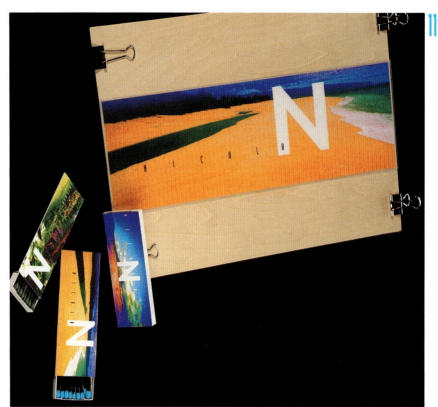
5

1. Poster design for a museum exhibit of graphic design.
2. Poster for AIGA Communication Graphics show.
3. Take out items packaging for Nicola Restaurant.
4. Nicola dinnerware.
5. Menus and matches.
6. Stationery system.

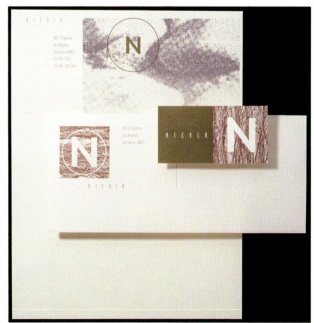
6

A P R I L   G R E I M A N ,   I N C .

1. Signage design for the Cerritos Center for the Performing Arts.
2.-4. Exterior tile design.
5. Interior tile design.
6. Logo for the center.
7. Patterning on glass balustrade.
8. Interior signage.
9. Textile design for auditorium seating.
10.-12. Computer generated signage imagery.

1

2

3

4

5

Cerritos Center for the Performing Arts

6

7

9

8

10

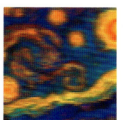

11

12

APRIL GREIMAN, INC.

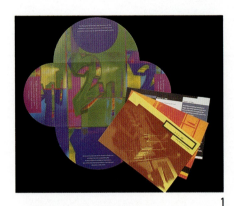

1. Fundraising brochure for Sci-Arc, Southern California Institute of Architecture.
2. Sci-Arc summer programs poster.
3. Sci-Arc continuing education booklet.
4.-6. Spreads from the student workbook, *from the edge.*
7. Stationery system.
8. Zap shot camera imagery for Sci-Arc student workbook.
9. Poster for the Museum of Modern Art.

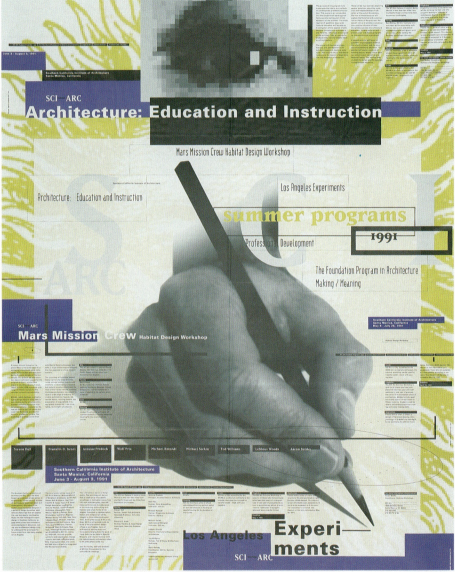

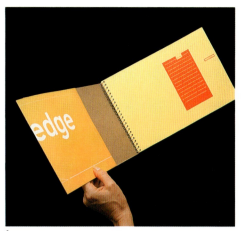

4

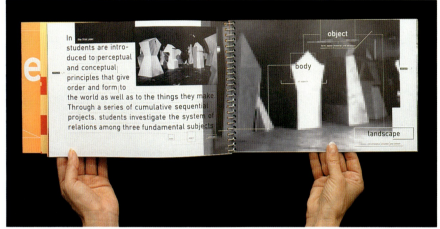

5

8

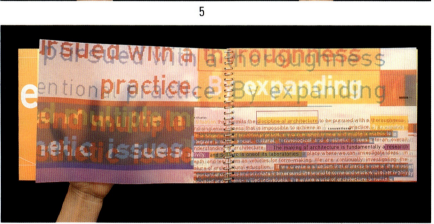

6

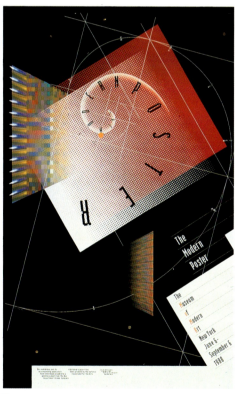

9

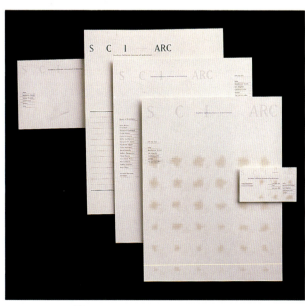

7

A P R I L   G R E I M A N ,   I N C .

620 Moulton #211   Los Angeles, CA 90031   213.227.1222   fax 213.2278651

124

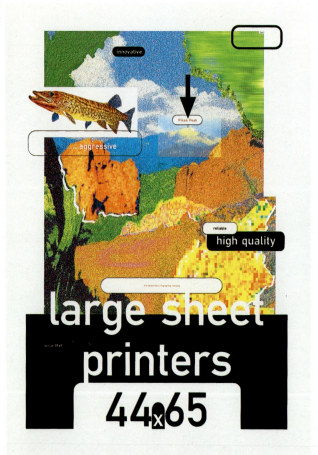

1. Poster for a printer.
2. Hang tags for a clothing manufacturer.
3. Underwear box packaging.

HARD WERKEN DESIGN

HARD WERKEN DESIGN

"You can be beautiful and stupid, or you can be beautiful and brilliant," asserts Dutch designer Henk Elenga of Hard Werken. "Our work is practical and effective in the good Dutch tradition." Elenga is both a furniture and graphic designer.

According to partner Rick Vermuelen, graphic design has to communicate quickly. He says, "If a poster is aesthetically constructed, but you have to read three books to understand it, that is ineffective design."

Elenga and Vermuelen staff the Hard Werken L.A. desk, which is an off-shoot of the innovative Rotterdam firm, Hard Werken Design. The Los Angeles office operates independently of its Dutch parent.

The firm develops publications, books, book covers, corporate identity systems, packaging and posters for clients in the United States and Europe. Their client list is diverse, tending toward arts and entertainment Vermuelen says, "A book is a product. The written part may be a work of art, but the jacket is a package. You have to make it work."

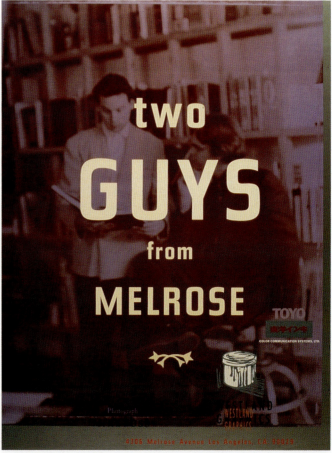

2

1

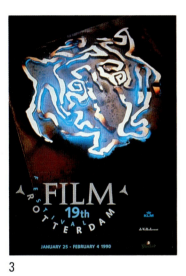

3

5

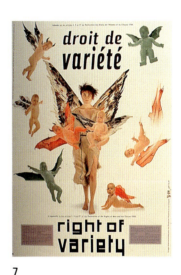

7

4

6

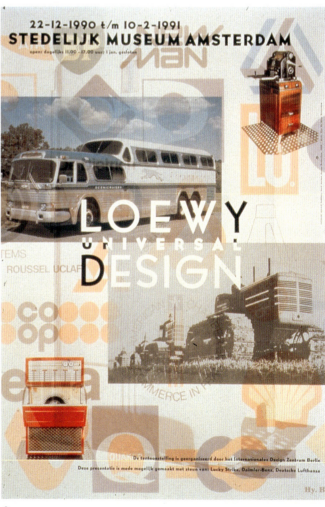

8

1. Studio identity.
2. Promotional poster for the studio.
3. Poster for a film festival.
4. Poster for a performance festival.
5. Poster for a sculpture exhibit in Italy.
6. Poster for an art show.
7. Bicentennial of human rights poster.
8. Poster for a museum exhibit.

1

1. Symbol for a children's clothing line.
2. Packaging and display design.
3.-4. Furniture design.
5. Light fixture design.
6. Forknife, designed as a promotional piece for an airline.
7. Catalog on the history of design created for the Dutch Postal Service, (PTT).
8.-9. Art exhibit catalogs.
10. Spread from a magazine on art and photography.
11. Book jacket design.

2

3

4

5

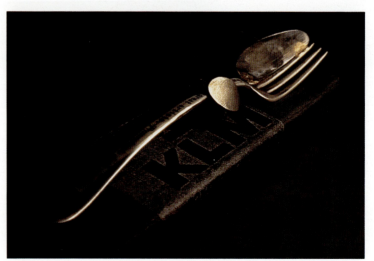

6

HARD WERKEN DESIGN

7

11

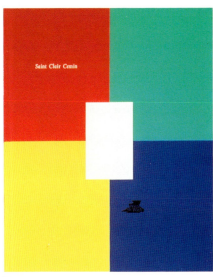

8

9

10

2

1

3

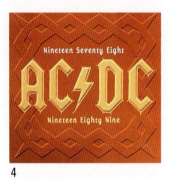
4

5

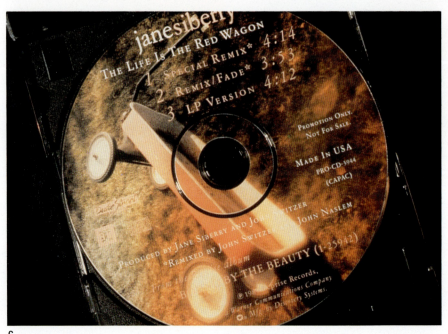
6

HARD WERKEN DESIGN

7

8

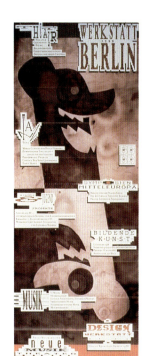

10

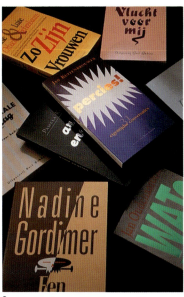

9

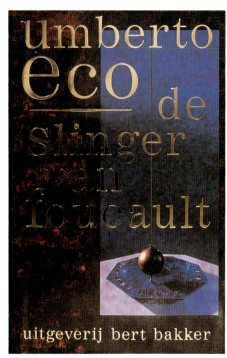

11

1. Logo for a recording company.
2.-6. CD packaging.
7. Dutch postage stamp design.
8. Identity for a design consulting firm.
9. Book jacket designs.
10. Poster design.
11. Book jacket design.

HARD WERKEN DESIGN

5514 Wilshire Blvd.   9th Floor   Los Angeles, CA 90036   213.9342186   fax213.938.7632

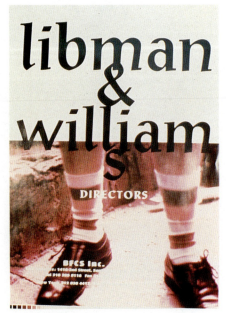

1. Advertisement for a trade magazine for directors.
2. Identity for a furniture store.
3.-4. Advertisements for a trade magazine for directors.

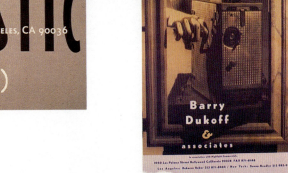

WAYNE HUNT DESIGN, INC.

WAYNE HUNT DESIGN, INC

Environmental graphic designer Wayne Hunt says,"We combine the classic principles of two-dimensional design with the three-dimensional world of architecture and environments." He's recently put those principles to work at theme parks and retail developments, such as Pleasure Island at Walt Disney World, Sanrio Puroland in Tokyo, and One Colorado in Old Pasadena.

Founded in 1977, the Pasadena-based company develops signage and graphics programs for office environments, retail spaces and public buildings and parks. The firm is actually geared for large scale projects like amusement parks. In fact, the larger the better. "We thrive on the bigger picture," explains Hunt. "Working on buildings and sites and projects that have some permanence and some sense of scale that is larger than us."

For Camp Snoopy, at the megamall, Mall of America, the firm designed original graphics for all the rides, attractions, stores, games and food operations as well as directional and operational signing. The whole package included over 300 original designs and 1,000 individual signs park-wide..

1

2

3

4

5

6

7

8

9

10

11

1. Wayne Hunt.
2. Icons developed for the signage program at Edmund D. Edelman Children's Court.
3. Symbol design.
4. Interior signage.
5. Icon as sculpture and level identification.
6. Interior signage.
7. Children's court theme mural.
8.-9. Interior signage.
10. Velcro wall sculpture.
11. Interior signage.

WAYNE HUNT DESIGN, INC

4

1

FunDazzle
2

5

6

3

1. Neon identification for a children's amusement/daycare center.
2. Logo design.
3. Traveling Bill of Rights exhibit designed for Unocal.
4.-6. Interior graphics.
7.-12. Signage for Camp Snoopy. A selection from the more than 250 signs created for this project.

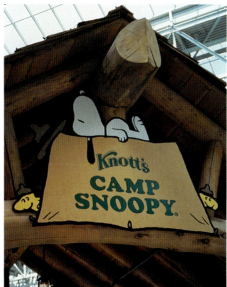
7

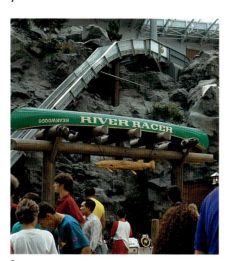
8

9

10

11

12

ONE COLORADO

1

2

3

DEVIL'S GATE

4

5

6

WAYNE HUNT DESIGN, INC

7

8

9

10

1. Symbol for a shopping center.
2. Logo for California Council of Interior Design Certification.
3. Symbol for University Children's Medical Group.
4. Symbol for a passive recreation park.
5. Fund raising brochure to save Frank Lloyd Wright's Innis-Brown House.
6. Marketing materials for an architectural firm.
7.- 8. Interior signage identification system for the California Mart.
9. Capabilities brochure for Video Image, a special effects house.
10. Stationery systems created for architectural firms.

WAYNE HUNT DESIGN, INC

87 N. Raymond #215   Pasadena, CA 91103   818.793.7847   fax 818.793.2549

1. Streetscape signage system created for Culver City.
2. Sign mock-up for evaluation.

L O O K I N G

LOOKING

Having spent six years in Europe and one year in Japan, Looking founder John Clark has built a design firm that truly is global in scope. In fact, after spending years in Switzerland consulting, teaching and working, the company maintains a presence there. "We have a printer in Switzerland as a client right now," Clark says. "I think it's because we are more involved with the marketing aspects than the Swiss."

Looking, founded in 1990, develops projects for a broad range of businesses and institutions. "We generally have fewer clients, but with many projects," the principal explains. "One client may require dozens of pieces, occurring over a time period of several years." Those pieces may include everything from corporate identity projects to exhibition displays to advertising to packaging or environments.

Clark, who has served as department chairman for the Communication Design Department at Art Center College of Design (Europe), enjoys teaching immensely. He currently teaches corporate design at Art Center, here.

A few years ago, when John was naming his firm, his goal was to choose an active verb. "Also, with a name like 'Looking', it could be anyone's office," he explains. "The format is such that anyone can rise to the top. It's fun. It's not as serious as Joe Smith and Associates, Inc."

1

2

3

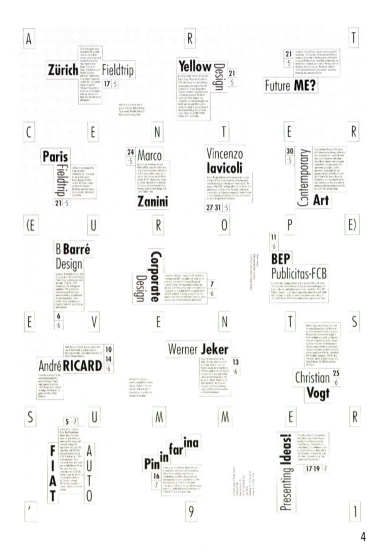

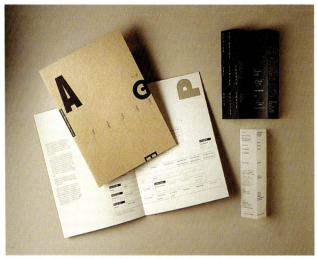
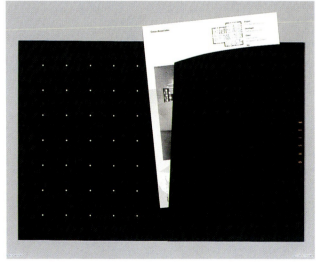

1. John Clark, Paul Langland and Marianne Thompson in the studio. (not shown, Laurent Tschumy)
2. Studio moving announcement.
3. Studio brochure.
4. Summer events poster for Art Center College of Design (Europe).
5. Studio promotion, "Looking" glasses.
6. Catalog for Art Center.
7. Presentation folder and project sheets for Onsite, an interior planning firm.

Indent

ABCDEFGHIJKLMNOPQRSTUVWXYZ
abcdefghijklmnopqrstuvwxyz
1234567890

1

2

3

4

LOOKING

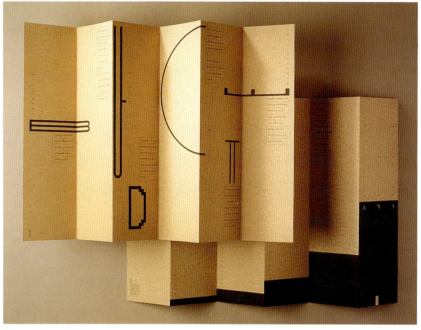

5

7

6

1. Typeface design.
2. Logotype and promotional materials for an event celebrating the founding of Futurism for the UCLA Italian department.
3. Identity for WestWeek, an event for the interior furnishings industry.
4. Brochure/program for WestWeek.
5. Brochure for a furniture manufacturer.
6. Logo for furniture manufacturer.
7. *New Questions* poster addressing the issues of print/production in an environmentally responsible manner.

LOOKING

146

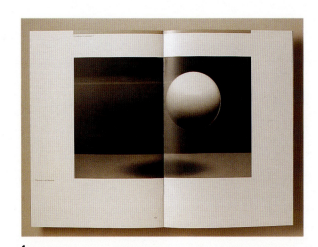
1

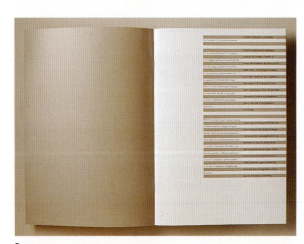
2

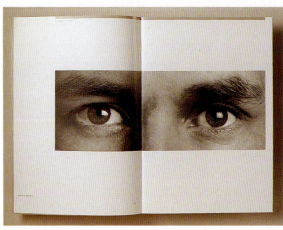
3

4

1.-3. Capabilities brochures for CAPCO Capacity Finance and Trading Companies.

4. Annual report for a food and drug retail company.

5.-6. Showroom exhibition and signing.

7. Product catalogs.

8. Product binder.

5

7

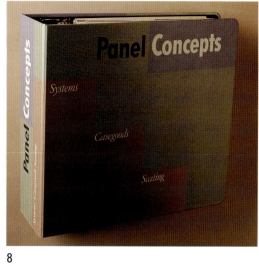

8

6

LOOKING

660 S. Avenue 21   Los Angeles, CA 90031   213.226.1086   fax 213.222.9170

148

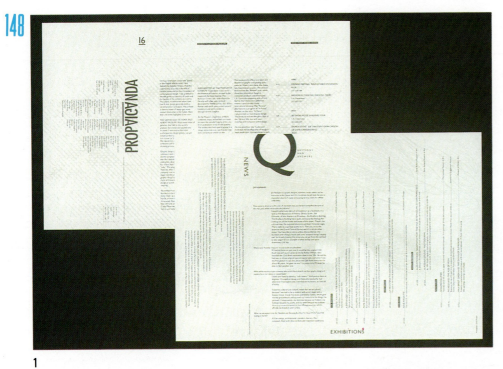

1

1. Newsletter for AIGA/LA.
2. Marketing materials for Panel Concepts.

2

LOUEY/RUBINO DESIGN GROUP

LOUEY/RUBINO DESIGN GROUP

Robert Louey and Regina Rubino, of Louey/Rubino Design Group, recently made plans to expand their offices to Jakarta and Hong Kong. That's a long way from where they met--as students at the New York High School of Art and Design.

After working as designers in New York for years, the two moved to California in 1987 to relocate their firm, which is now headquartered in Santa Monica. "Robert had always wanted to live in California," says Regina. "So when one of our biggest clients in New York, MGM, relocated everyone to their studio in Culver City, we made the move, too. It was a way to move here and have a client right away."

The company, which handles corporate design, packaging, environmental space planning, marketing and public relations, has always had a presence internationally, working in France and Italy, for example. While both designers are involved in every project, Regina handles more of the administrative and management duties. "We're very excited about our entry into the Asian market," she says.

PHOTO: BURTON PRITZKER

1

1. Regina Rubino and Robert Louey.
2.-4. Studio self-promotion, "The Art of Communication".
5. Identity for a florist.

2

3

4

Fleurs du Jour
2525 Main Street
Santa Monica, California 90405
213-399-9131

5

LOUEY/RUBINO DESIGN GROUP

1

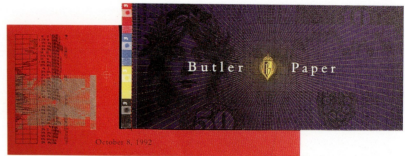

4

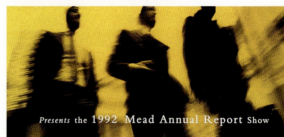

5

6

2

3

1. Quarterly publication for an accounting firm.

2.-3. International Space year calendar, designed to celebrate the 500th anniversary of Columbus' voyage.

4.-6. Invitation to an exhibit of annual reports for a paper distributor.

7. Portfolio and calendar promotion for a printer.

LOUEY/RUBINO DESIGN GROUP

1

2

3

4

5

6

7

8

9

1. Symbol for Desk Talk Systems, Inc.
2. Symbol for Panda-Monium, a gift shop.
3. Symbol for a film producer who focuses on spiritual films of the American West.
4. Symbol for Davide Fur Salon.
5. Logo for the popular cartoon characters for use on merchandise and licensing materials.
6.-7. Brochure/press kit for a menswear manufacturer.
8.-9. Capabilities brochure for a real estate investment company.
10. Brochure for a building products manufacturer.
11.-12. Capabilities brochure for Rockwell International Corporation.

LOUEY/RUBINO DESIGN GROUP

2525 Main Street #204   Santa Monica, CA 90405   310.396.7724   fax 310.396.1686

1

2

3

1. Environmental design, signing and logo for Unlimited Pastabilities Restaurant.
2. Banner design for Sichuan Court Restaurant.
3. Environmental design for Sichuan Court Restaurant.

MADDOCKS & COMPANY

MADDOCKS & COMPANY

From fragrances to computers, Maddocks & Company handles collateral packaging, product design, corporate identity and point-of-purchase systems for a broad base of clients.

The common thread in all their projects is their principle goal--helping the client move product. "We design to help our clients sell," principal Frank Maddocks says. "We just did a super-market private brand of coffee. It's become the number one selling coffee in the store. That's what I like to hear."

While Maddocks, whose firm also has an office in New York, handles management and sales, the creative end of the business is overseen by creative director Mary Scott. "Awards are important to us as designers," she says. "But to us, the real award is a successful product and having the client come back again and again."

2

3

4

1. Maddocks & Company.
2. Holiday packaging.
3. Collateral program for a cellular phone company.
4. Product design.

MADDOCKS & COMPANY

1

3

2

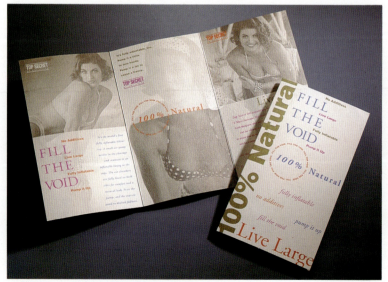

4

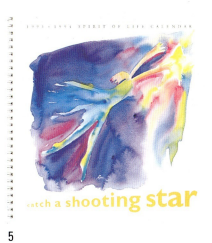
5

3

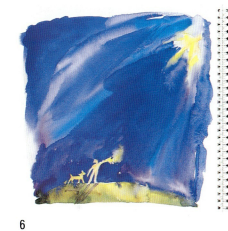
6

1. Tenth anniversary packaging and Limoges box for Giorgio Beverly Hills.
2.-3. Product design and packaging for fragrance lines.
4. Introductory brochure for inflatable swimwear.
5.-7. Commemorative calendar for City of Hope hospital.
8. Packaging for computer accessories line.
9. Bottle design for a new fragrance.

7

8

9

162

MADDOCKS & COMPANY

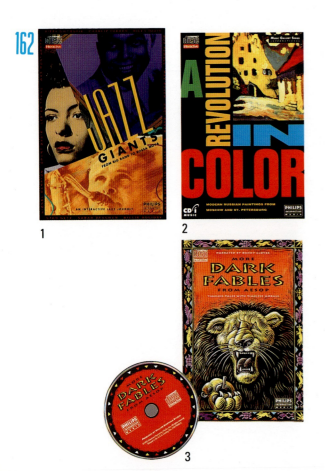

1

2

3

4

5

6

1.-3. Packaging for interactive CDs.
4. Men's cologne packaging.
5. Collateral materials for Philips Interactive Media of America.
6. Toy packaging.
7. Point of purchase display.
8.-9. New product press kits.
10. Supermarket identity.
11. Logo for a furniture store.
12. Logo for a fragrance.
13. Symbol for private label barbeque packaging.
14. Symbol for food vending machine company.
15. Symbol for women's boxer shorts manufacturer.

10

11

12

8

9

13

14

15

MADDOCKS & COMPANY

2011 Pontius Avenue   Los Angeles, CA 90025   310.477.4227   fax 310.479.5767

164

1.-2. Market private label packaging.
3. Point of purchase display.

NORMAN MOORE/DESIGN ART, INC.

NORMAN MOORE/DESIGN ART, INC.

"A lot of times my first instincts are what please me most," designer Norman Moore says. "There's a thrill about working fast, which is something I learned when I was working with Rod Dyer many years ago."

Moore, who is a native of Scotland, studied graphic design at Harrow School of Art in London and worked at two London design firms before moving to California in 1972. He spent two years working with the Rod Dyer Group, moved back to London, then came back to California in 1977 to work at MCA Records as art director. Moore opened DesignArt in 1979.

The firm develops corporate identity, annual reports, packaging, publication design, posters, book jackets and record covers for a client base that largely consists of entertainment and high-tech companies. "I'd like to be doing more corporate work," Moore says. "In fact, it's good for my corporate clients when I inject a bit of humor in their work.

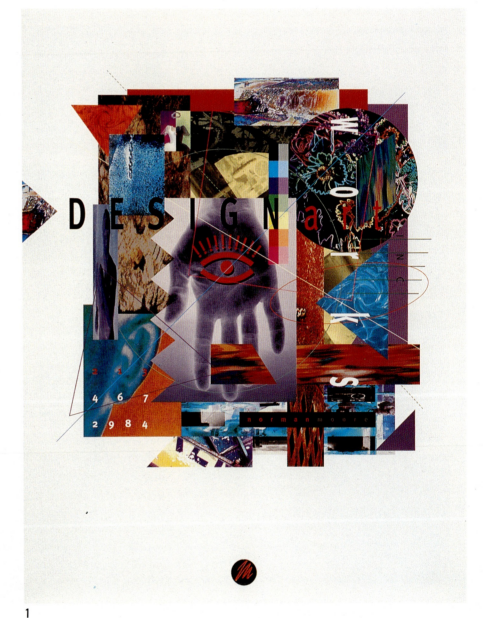

1. Promotional piece for the studio.
2.-3 CD packaging.
4. Stationery system.
5. Poster for Capitol Records.

2

3

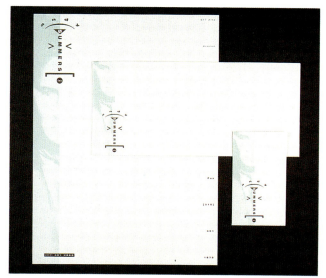
4

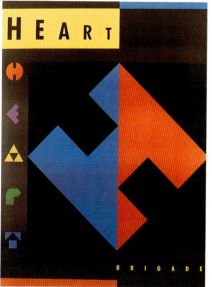
5

NORMAN MOORE/DESIGN ART, INC.

1

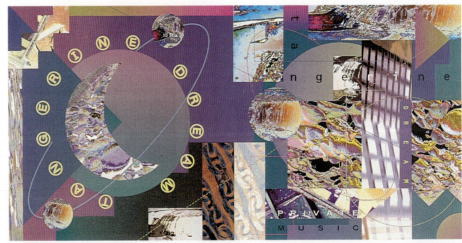

2

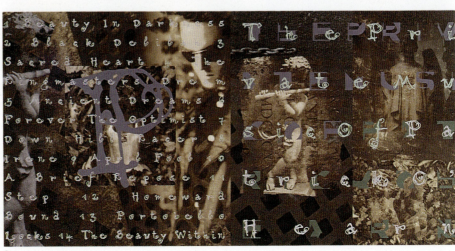

3

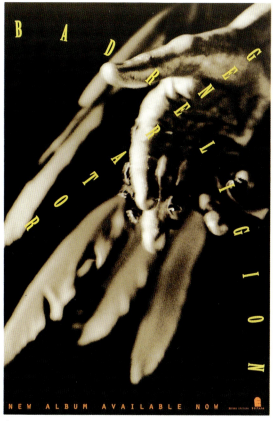

4

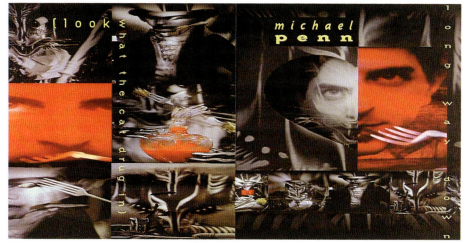

5

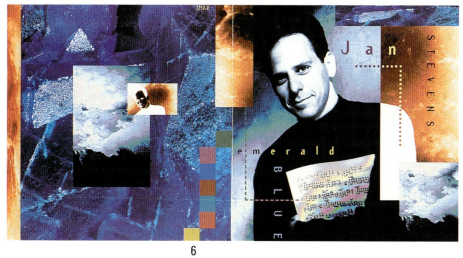

6

7

1. CD packaging.
2. CD enclosure booklet.
3. CD enclosure booklet for The Private Music of Patrick O'Hearn.
4. Poster for a recording company.
5.-6. CD enclosure booklets.
7. Human rights poster for the Humanitas Foundation.

NORMAN MOORE/DESIGN ART, INC.

1

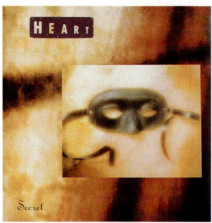
4

2

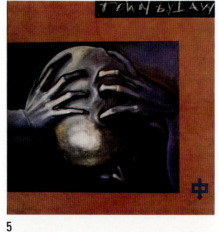
5

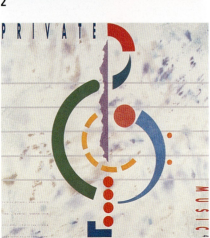
3

6

1. CD packaging.
2. CD packaging.
3. Album cover
4.-5 Album cover design.
6. Packaging of a 12" single record.
7. Symbol for FM Productions, a film production company.
8. Symbol for Digital Design Centre, a computer graphics bureau.
9. Symbol for QuickMaid, a coffee vending service.
10. Symbol for Braverman Film Production Company.
11. Symbol for Film Star, a film production company.
12. Symbol for Digital Arts, a computer graphics software company.
13. Symbol for Tim Neece Management.
14. Symbol for Westbeach Recording Studio.
15. Symbol for Libman/Moore Video Production Company.

7

10

13

8

11

14

9

12

15

NORMAN MOORE/DESIGN ART, INC.

6311 Romaine #7311   Los Angeles, CA 90038   213.467.2984   fax 213.467.1985

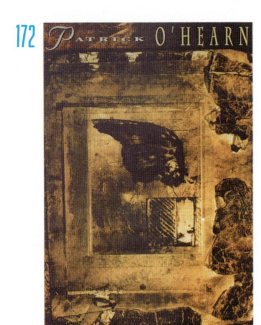

1

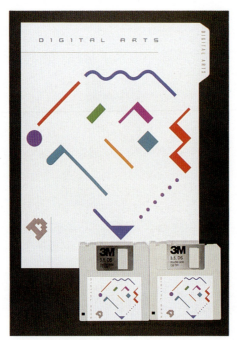

2

3

4

1. Poster for Private Music.
2. Press kit and floppy disk labels for Digital Arts.
3. CD enclosure booklet.
4. Self-promotional Syquest Cartridge cover.

Ph.D

O PICTURES
1

2

3

JOHNNY LOVE'S
4

5

MIND OVER MACINTOSH
6

7

8

When English designers Clive Piercy and Michael Hodgson went into partnership in January 1988, they were going to call themselves The Knowledge. Michael explains, "It's the two-year training that London cab drivers go through to learn every street in the city. You see them driving around on mopeds with clipboards attached to the handlebars. They have to know if a street is one-way, two-way or has a cul-de-sac."

"When we went into partnership," Michael continues, "we decided we would be designers who would really think about projects and learn what the clients needed, that's why we wanted to use the name, 'The Knowledge'." But then a photographer friend convinced them to go with initials. "Like the big ad agencies—JWT," recalls Michael. "We settled on Ph.D, not because they happen to be our initials but because it stands for knowledge."

In the beginning, the Santa Monica-based firm worked mostly in music. Piercy explains,"But now we're also doing fashion, galleries, restaurants, that sort of thing." "Recently, the firm developed graphics for Nike, AT&T and Xerox television commercials. "It was very exciting," says Clive. "One of the AT&T spots was about the future of technology. That technology didn't exist, so we had to make it up."

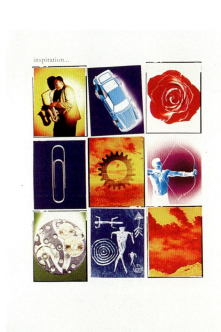

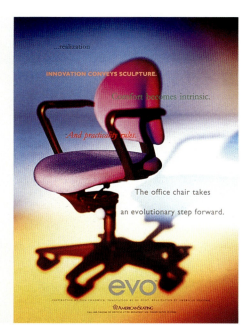

12

1. Symbol for O Pictures.
2. Logo for a product design company.
3. Logo for Evelyne Penia, fashion designer.
4. Logo for a restaurant.
5. Logo for Raisins, a swimwear manufacturer.
6. Mind Over Macintosh logo, a company that provides Mac training.
7. Logo for Montana Artists, agents for film technicians.
8. Symbol for an advertising agency.
9. Drawing of Michael and Clive.
10.-11. Marketing and advertising for the launch of an ergonomic office chair.
12. Logo for the EVO chair.

Ph.D

1

2

1. Brochure for an exercise studio.
2. Logo for MIX, a shopping complex.
3. Promotional packaging for MIX.
4. Packaging for Elika products.
5. Swimwear advertisement.
6. Mail order fashion catalog.
7. Advertisement for a photographer.
8. Advertisement for a fund raising event.
9. Announcement for an art gallery.
10. Artist's promotion.

3

4

5

6

7

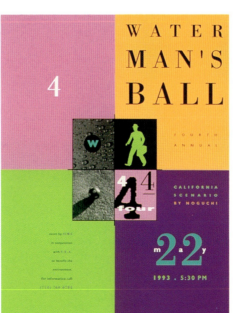
8

9

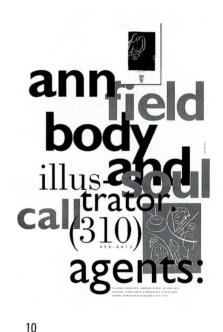
10

7

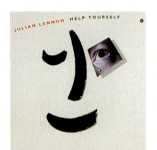

1

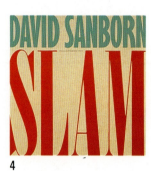

4

1.-6. Album or CD covers.
7. Symbol for a record label.
8. CD packaging for a jazz series.
9. Tags and labeling for Steel Jeans.
10. Book design.
11. Stationery system for an illustrator.
12. Swimwear advertisement.

2

5

3

6

8

Ph.D

11

10

12

P h . D

1524A Cloverfield   Santa Monica, 90404   310.829.0900   fax 310.829-1859

1

2

3

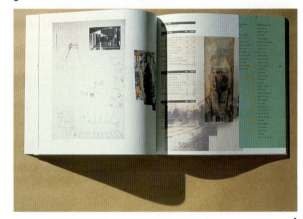

4

1.-2. Art direction and design for AT&T commercials.
3.-4. Cover and spread from a prospectus for an art school.

SARGENT & BERMAN

SARGENT & BERMAN

Peter Sargent and Greg Berman met eleven years ago while working at Bright & Associates. "We worked on a lot of projects together and after five years decided to form a partnership," explains Greg Berman. Along with a staff of designers, the two develop corporate identity, packaging, collateral and signage for clients in health care, travel, entertainment, packaged goods and restaurants.

Of their partnership, Greg says, "We have a good balance between us--a strong marketing sense and strong creative ability." While Berman functions more as an art director, Peter takes over on the design aspects. The two work on or oversee each project that comes in, and attend all creative presentations.

"One thing we learned a long time ago," Berman says, "is that, as professionals, design solutions usually develop quickly. It's the day-to day business side of what we do that really demands our attention-- making sure the clients are happy and watching cash flow. If you want success, a good business sense becomes as important as producing great design."

SARGENT
& BERMAN

183

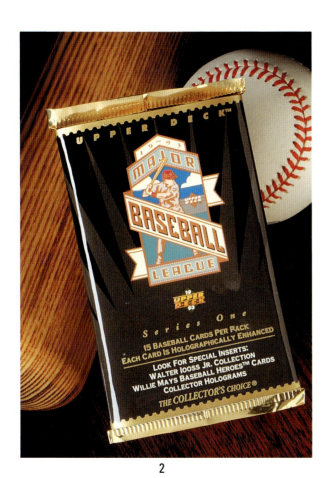

2

3

4

5

6

1. Product labeling and package design.
2-5. Packaging and point of purchase display for a trading card manufacturer.
6. Packaging and accompanying study guide for Worldlink, a video magazine for secondary schools.

SARGENT & BERMAN

1

2

1.-2. Catalog for a cycling clothing manufacturer.

3. Product development and packaging of a system of decorations for children's rooms.

4. Cruise brochure system.

5. Identity for The Regal Princess and materials created for its inaugural cruise.

6. Holiday banners created for the city of Beverly Hills.

7. Pen and pencil set packaging.

8. Promotional mailer to introduce a line of Coca-Cola clothing.

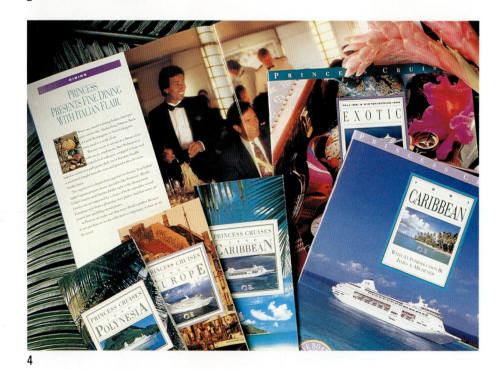

4

3

5

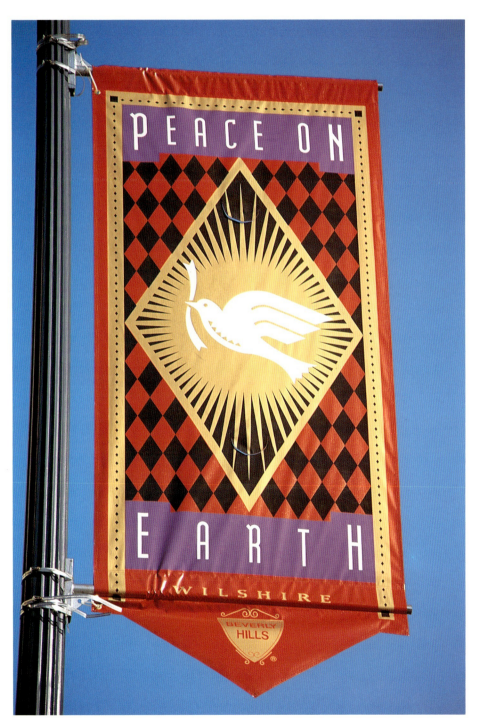

6

7

8

SARGENT & BERMAN

1. Identity for a company that leads team building workshops for corporations.
2. Identity for a company that provides management and accounting services to the healthcare industry.
3.- 4. Maternity care capabilities brochure.
5. Symbol and stationery system for Outerspace, a digital retouching service.
6. Packaging for a line of office products made from recycled plastics.
7. Packaging for a children's clothing store.
8. Symbol for a printer.
9. Symbol for a supper club.
10. Symbol for a travel consultant.
11.-12. Logos for Venture Up activities.

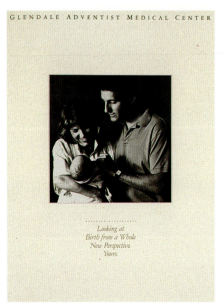

5

6

7

ANDERSON
PRINTING

8

MOGULS

9

APA Travel Center

10

11

12

SARGENT & BERMAN

1237A Third St.   Santa Monica, CA 90401   310.576.1070   fax 310.5761074

1

1. Folder containing a printer's post script service information.
2. Food packaging for snack bars.

2

SHIFFMAN YOUNG DESIGN GROUP

SHIFFMAN YOUNG DESIGN GROUP

"Truly great design leaves no fingerprints." That's the creative philosophy behind Shiffman Young Design Group. Founded in 1985, Tracey Shiffman and Roland Young work from a client list that includes arts organizations, healthcare companies, book publishers, schools, museums and foundations.

Shiffman, who trained at the California Institute of the Arts, serves as art director, graphic designer and group business administrator. Her goal is to deliver concise, uncomplicated design solutions. "Spare, clean, original design is what we do best," she says.

Designer Roland Young is known for his work in album cover and billboard design in the sixties and seventies. He attended the California College of Arts and Crafts and the Chouinard Institute. He then graduated from Art Center College of Design, where he now teaches.

The two partners, along with designer Meryl Pollen, develop brochures, books, posters, trademark identity systems and CD covers. "We have an old-fashioned design consciousness," says Shiffman. "We don't allow the computer to drive our work. We don't allow illustration or photography to drive our work. We drive it"

1

2

3

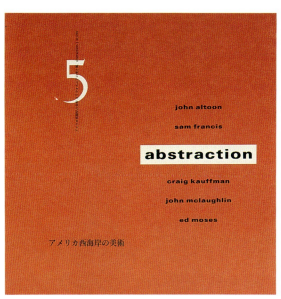

1. Tracey Shiffman, Roland Young, Meryl Pollen and Spider.
2. Symbol, identity for the studio
3. Series of booklets for the Frederick Weisman Art Foundation.
4. Poster for the Getty Center for the History of Art and the Humanities Fellowship Program.
5. Catalog for an exhibit at the Nagoya City Art Museum.

SHIFFMAN YOUNG DESIGN GROUP

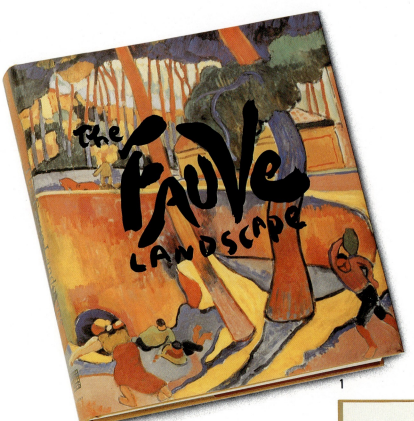

1.-9. Catalog/book for the Los Angeles County Museum of Art exhibition, *The Fauve Landscape*.

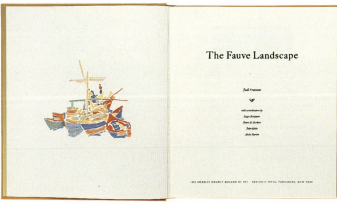

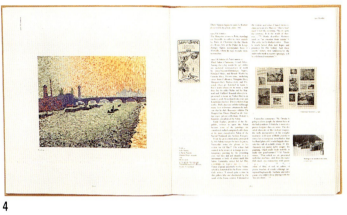

4

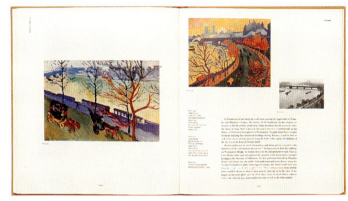

7

5

8

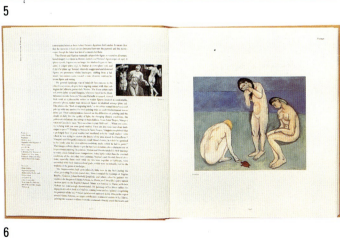

6

9

SHIFFMAN YOUNG DESIGN GROUP

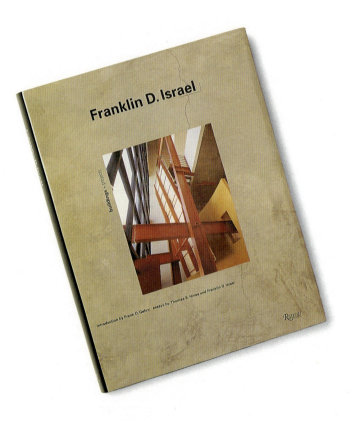

1.-8. Book design for the Rizzoli architectural monograph series.

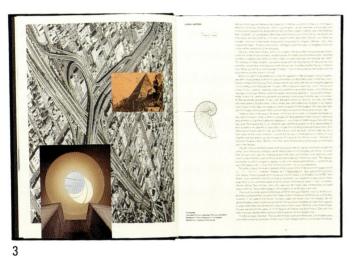

3

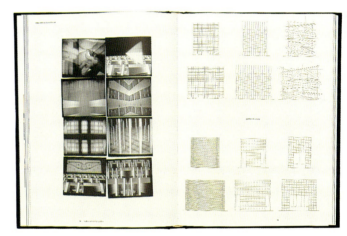

6

7

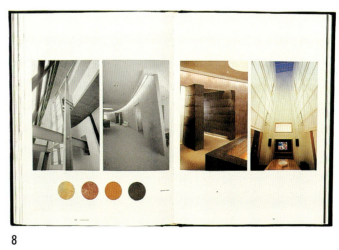

8

SHIFFMAN YOUNG DESIGN GROUP

7421 Beverly Boulevard #4   Los Angeles, CA 90025   213.930.1816   fax 213.930.1056

196

Biannual publication for the Getty Center for Education in the Arts. DBAE, Disciplined Based Art Education.

SHIMOKOCHI/REEVES

SHIMOKOCHI/REEVES

Established in 1985, Shimokochi/Reeves is a design firm that prides itself in becoming marketing partners with its clients. "In certain cases, a client will call us when they're conceptualizing their product," principal Anne Reeves explains. "They want our unbiased feedback because we understand their marketing objectives."

Although both principals are designers, Mamoru Shimokochi immerses himself in the creative side while Reeves handles the management aspects of the firm. "I'm very involved in project management—meeting with clients," she says. "But Mamoru and I also work as a team on the creative."

Shimokochi, who was born in Japan and has lived in the United States for over 30 years, spent seven years working at Saul Bass & Associates as senior designer. Born and educated in England, Reeves also worked as a designer at Saul Bass, following extensive design experience in London.

The two are very focused on the success of their clients' products. One of their projects, a packaging system for DEP Corporation's L.A. Looks hair care products, helped to sell fifty million units in only four years without any advertising. "We don't design for the sake of design," says Shimokochi. "The packaging has to sell the product."

1

4

2

5

6

7

Tokyo Broadcasting System
8

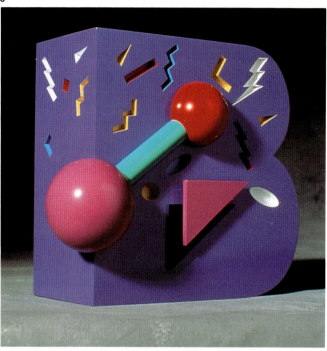
9

10

11

1. Mamoru Shimokochi.
2. The studio.
3. Self-promotional poster.
4. Anne Reeves.
5. Tracy McGoldrick, Anne Reeves, Nobuo Hirano, Mamoru Shimokochi, and Ingrid Konupek.
6. Tokyo Broadcasting System exterior signage.
7. Billboards placed throughout Tokyo.
8. Logo.
9. Proposed outdoor signage.
10. Station identification sequence.
11. Stationery system.

SHIMOKOCHI/REEVES

1

2

3

1. Stationery system and desk accessories for the UCLA School of Theater, Film & Television.

2. Gift items for the school.

3. Coffee mugs for the UCLA Graduate School of Library & Information Science.

4. Symbol for UCLA Graduate School of Library & Information Science.

5. Trademark for the Good Shepherd Dental Laboratory.

6. Identity for Mingtai Insurance Company, Taiwan.

7. Symbol for a Japanese recording company.

8. Trademark for Healing Arts, a production company specializing in physical awareness videos.

9. Logo for an Australian interior design and planning company.

10. Symbol for World Children's Baseball Fair, an international organization that unites children through baseball.

11. Trademark for a line of golf apparel.

12. Logo for a manufacturer of computer components.

4

7

10

5

8

11

6

9

12

1.-2. Proposed corporate identity and application for Hankyu Railroad, Japan.

3. Packaging for a line of hair care products.

4. Package identity for fast food products.

5. Product development for a line of youth-oriented hair care products.

6. Packaging for a line of specialty foods.

7. Package and brand identity for a line of Mexican food.

8. Logo for food packaging.

5

6

7

8

SHIMOKOCHI/REEVES

4465 Wilshire Boulevard   Los Angeles, CA 90010   213.937.3414   fax 213.937.3417

204

1

2

3

1. Annual forecast reports for First Interstate Bank.
2. Detail of cover illustration of forecast.
3. Poster design.

SIEGEL & GALE/CROSS

SIEGEL & GALE/CROSS

1

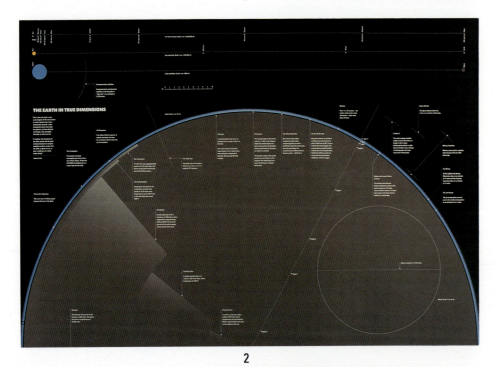

2

3

An international network of design offices in locations from Hong Kong to London to New Zealand, Siegel & Gale, headquartered in New York, is known for simple, compelling corporate and brand identity. And its Los Angeles office is no exception.

Headed by managing and creative director James Cross, Siegel and Gale/Cross turns out concise, elegant executions for clients including Acura, DuPont, EuroDisney, Simpson Paper, and Caterpillar, Inc among others. The firm has won numerous awards and international attention for its work in annual reports, collateral, and corporate identity.

In 1991, Cross was recipient of the Lifetime Achievement Award by the Art Directors Club of Los Angeles. He has served on the Board of Directors of the Aspen Design Conference and the American Institute of Graphic Arts (AIGA) in New York. Cross has also served as president of the Alliance Graphique Internationale.

Cross, who is a painter and printmaker, enjoys the creative challenges of the business. "Ideas that work," he says, "are those conceptual connections that not only deliver the message powerfully but make it understood, as well."

4

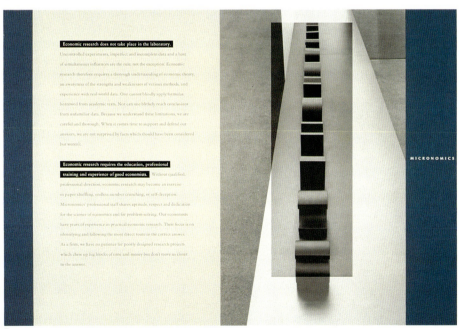
5

1. The studio
2.-3. Insert poster for a paper company self-promotion, *The Design of the Earth*.
4.-5. Capabilities brochure for Micronomics.
6. Identity for Acura.

6

SIEGEL & GALE/CROSS

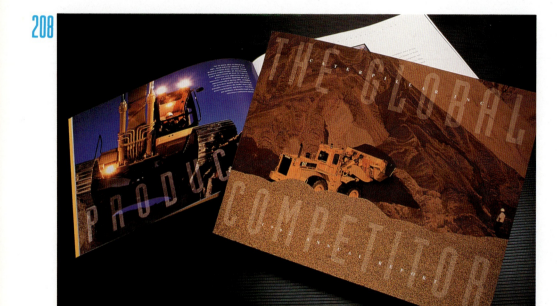

1

2

1. Annual report for Caterpiller.
2. Poster for a printer.
3. Logo for an upscale Chinese delivery restaurant.
4. Event identity.
5. Logo for a Japanese film company.
6. Symbol for a real estate development.
7. Logo for a paper manufacturer's magazine devoted to innovation and discovery.
8. Event identity for the LA Philharmonic.
9. Symbol for Resource Systems, a management consulting firm.
10. Identity for a restaurant.
11. Event identity.
12. Retail brand identity for food franchise.
13. Symbol for a group of editorial photographers.
14. Identity for *Ideas '92*, an Australian design conference.

3

7

11

4

8

12

5

9

13

6

10

14

SIEGEL & GALE/CROSS

210

1.-2. *Silverado*, promotional brochure for a paper manufacturer.
3. Simpson Paper Company's *Neo* magazine.
4.-6. Annual report for NCR Corporation.

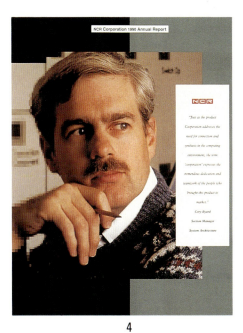

SIEGEL & GALE/CROSS

3465 W. 6th Street #300   Los Angeles, CA 90020   213.389.1010   fax 213.389.0064

212

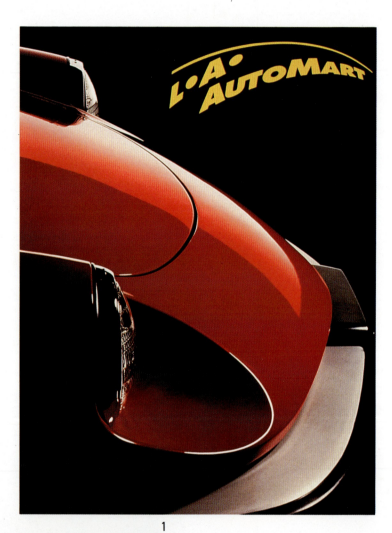

1.-2. Brochure for a real estate development whose focus is car sales.

PATRICK SOOHOO DESIGNERS

PATRICK SOOHOO DESIGNERS

"We're really a cross between a graphic design studio and a promotions agency," explains Patrick SooHoo. "An example would be a client who wants to do a sales incentive program. We develop marketing-based solutions with design principals and apply them to the whole project: poster, brochure, direct mail pieces and packaging."

Patrick SooHoo Designers has found its niche in producing full promotional packages as well as identity, packaging, collateral and advertising. "Our designers are very versatile," says SooHoo. "Because of the wide variety of projects we create, our designers have to be good with traditional design application, as well as being very adept with the computer."

The firm, founded by Patrick in 1976, services a diverse group of clients, ranging from entertainment to consumer goods to financial. Patrick's goal for all his clients is the same: "We're interested in conceptualizing, in getting to the solution. Making the work look good is easy. We like to solve the client's communcation problems."

1

2

1. Patrick SooHoo.
2. Self-promotional poster.
3.-5. Annual report for Los Angeles County Transportation Commission.

PATRICK SOOHOO DESIGNERS

216

1

2

3

1. Logo for Cabo San Lucas tourism board.
2. Stationery for an ITT Hartford/Elar Partners insurance company sales incentive program.
3. Announcement for the above program.
4.-5. Package design and identity for a line of skin care products.
6. Shopping bags for the Los Angeles County Music Center.

PATRICK SOOHOO DESIGNERS

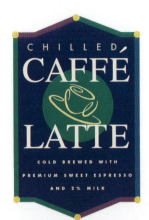

1

2

3

1. Logo and packaging identity for Toddy Products.
2. Symbol for National Advertising Golfers Association.
3. Licensing style guide for Walt Disney's *101 Dalmations*.
4.-5. Collateral material for ITT Hartford/Elar Partners sales incentive program.

219

4

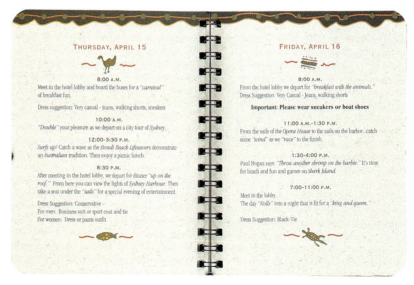

5

PATRICK SOOHOO DESIGNERS

8800 Venice Boulevard   Los Angeles, CA 90034   310.836.8800   fax 310.839.3039

1

4

7

5

8

3

9

1.-9. Rubber stamp graphics for Sizzler's international salad bar promotion.

SOS : LOS ANGELES

SoS: Los Angeles

"Most clients come to me because they're looking for unexpected solutions," says Susan Silton, principal of SoS Los Angeles. The firm, which was founded in 1986, specializes in servicing the needs of arts institutions and arts-related corporations.

"The challenge, even with the freedom such clients allow," she explains, "is to be inventive--even dazzling--as well as sensitive to the client's marketing strategy. A piece which on the surface reads beautifully but fundamentally ignores a client's needs is not successfully doing its job."

Silton's work has won numerous design awards and is included in the Library of Congress' permanent collection. She teaches in the Communication Design department at Art Center College of Design. She is also a fine artist who has shown at galleries and institutions throughout Los Angeles. As for the name of her studio, she prefers to keep its true meaning a mystery. "But," she reveals, "I will say 'o' is not my middle initial."

PHOTO: MERLYN ROSENBERG
1

2

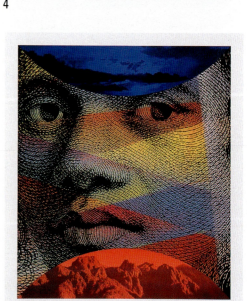
4

3

5

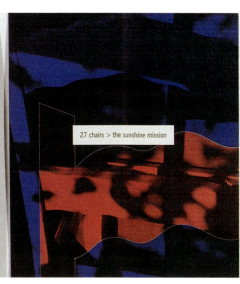

6

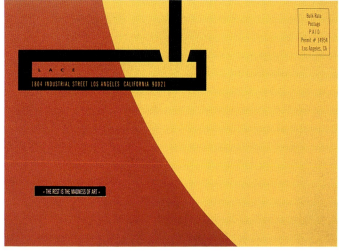

7   8

1. Susan Silton.
2.-5. Year-end self-promotional cards.
6. Invitation to a benefit auction.
7. Catalog for an art gallery exhibit.
8. Brochure for an art gallery.

SoS: LOS ANGELES

224

1

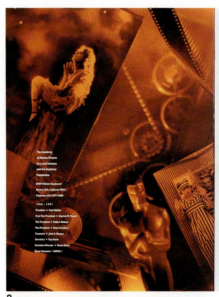
2

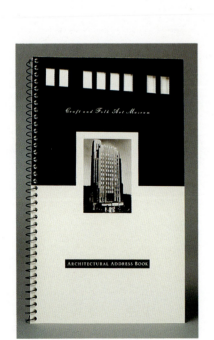
3

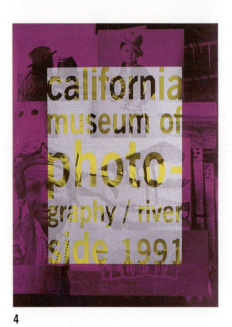
4

5

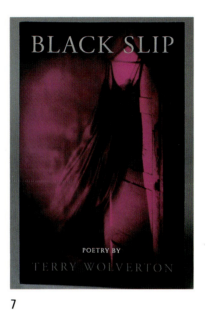

1.-2. Annual report for the Academy of Motion Picture Arts and Sciences and Academy Foundation.

3. Address book to benefit the Craft & Folk Art Museum.

4. Poster for the California Museum of Photography.

5. Museum poster/announcement.

6. 30th birthday party invitation.

7. Bookcover design.

8. Poster for The Getty Center for the History of Art and the Humanities.

6   7

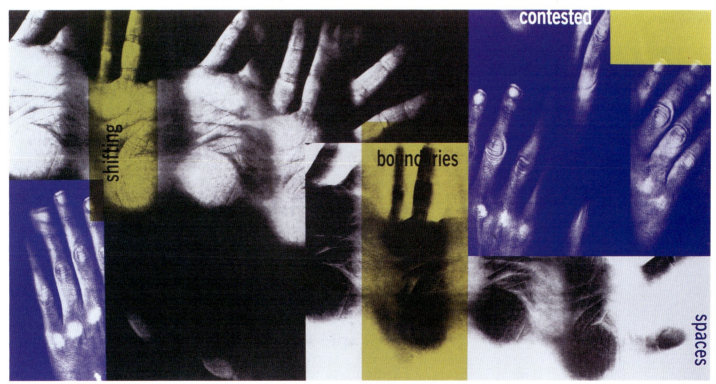

8

SoS: LOS ANGELES

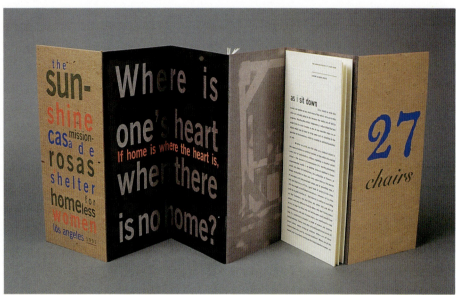

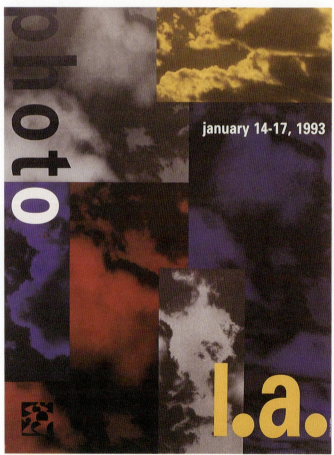

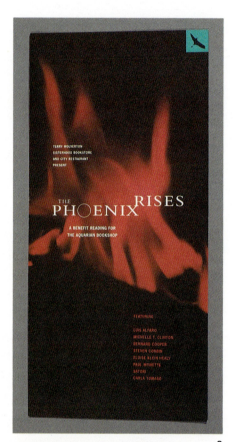

1. Benefit auction catalog.
2. Poster for the photo exposition Photo: L.A.
3. Postcard for fundraiser to benefit a bookstore burned in the Los Angeles riots.
4. Catalog cover for a publisher.
5. Catalog for an installation at the Museum of Contemporary Art.
6. Brochure for the Far Eastern Art Council, Los Angeles County Museum of Art.

4

5

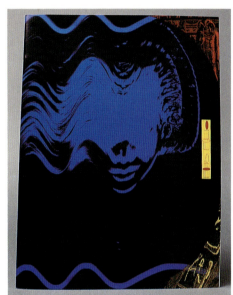
7

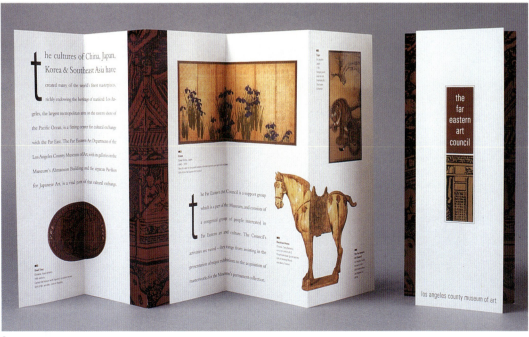
6

SoS: LOS ANGELES

3359 Garden Avenue   Los Angeles, CA 90039   213.660.4588   fax 213.660.3247

1

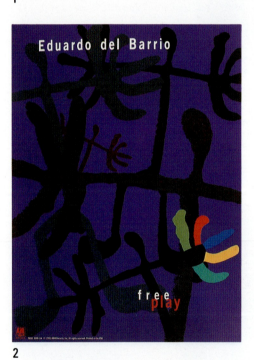

2

3

4

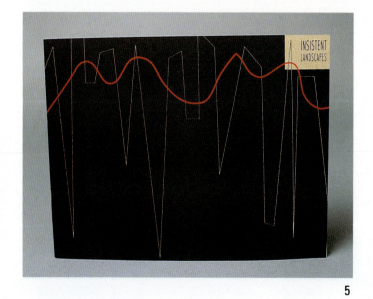

5

1. Postcard for Susan Silton exhibition.
2. Poster, one in a series of album packaging materials, for A&M records.
3. Brochure for American Society for Technion.
4. Exhibition brochure for the California Museum of Photography.
5. Exhibition catalog for Security Pacific Gallery.

SUSSMAN/PREJZA & CO, INC.

SUSSMAN/PREJZA & CO, INC.

Internationally known for their large scale urban design projects, the married team of environmental designer Deborah Sussman and architect Paul Prejza represent a true union of two disciplines.

In what has been dubbed "urban enhancement", the firm has actually defined a new approach to environmental design-- a collaboration of clients, planners, architects and graphic designers to rework city streets and buildings. One of their most visible examples of this discipline was the 1984 Summer Olympic Games, for which the firm created the look and organized a team that included well over 100 participating architects and designers.

Sussman, who is an enthusiastic student of folk art and regional styles, is an elected member of the Alliance Graphique Internationale and founded the Los Angeles chapter of the AIGA. She is an honorary member of the American Institute of Architects. An architect by training, Prezja has taught at the University of Southern California School of Architecture and has lectured at several colleges and universities.

In 1988, Sussman/Prejza & Company was awarded AIA Institute Honors, the highest recognition given by the AIA to a related profession.

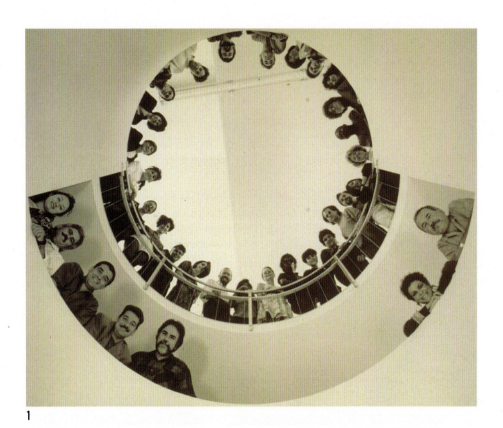
1

2

3

4

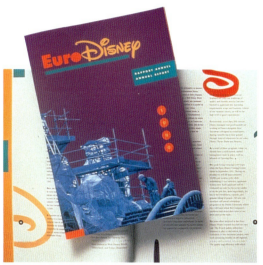

1. Sussman/Prejza staff.
2.-4. Trolley stop designs for the city of San Diego.
5. Catalog for UCLA continuing education.
6. Annual report for EuroDisney.
7. Poster for the Australia Tourist Commission.
8.-10. Signing and identity for a corporate park.

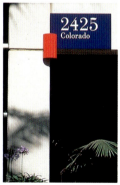
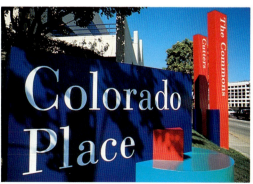
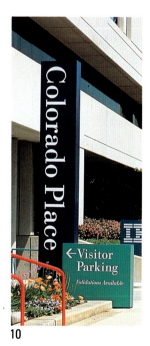

SUSSMAN/PREJZA & CO, INC.

1

2

3

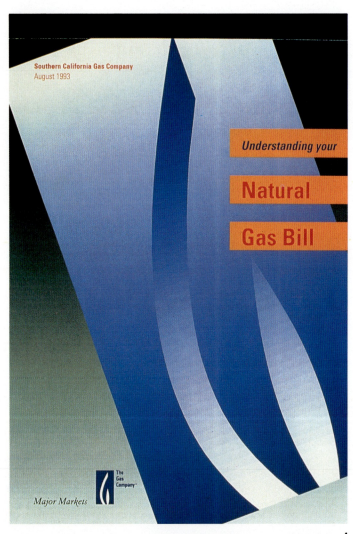
4

1.-2. Vehicle graphics for The Gas Company.
3. Newsletter.
4. Brochure for major markets.
5. Poster design.
6. Stationery system.
7. Uniform design.
8.-9. Environmental brochures.
10. Pocket calendar and pen.

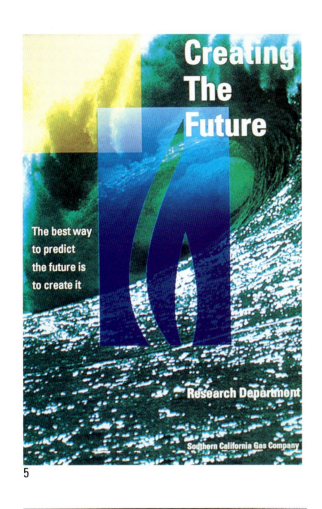
5

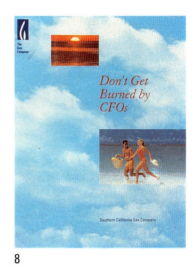
8

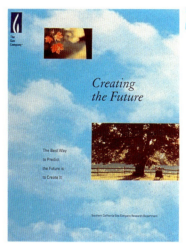
9

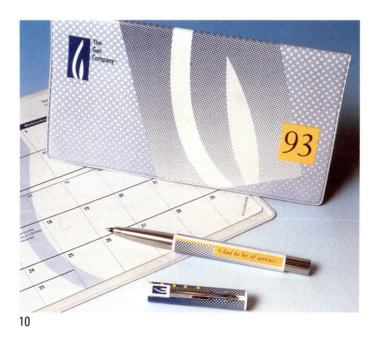
6

10

7

SUSSMAN/PREJZA & CO, INC.

234

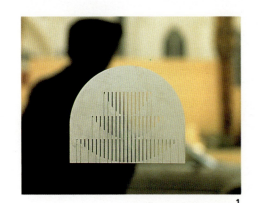

1

2

3

4

5

1. Symbol for Plaza Las Fuentes, a mixed use development, etched on entry door.
2.-5. Building identification signing.
4. Tile Graphics.
6.-7. Tenant signage in a shopping complex.
8.-9. Neon graphic on street bridge connecting shopping complex with an office park.

SUSSMAN/PREJZA & CO, INC.

3960 Ince Boulevard   Culver City, CA 90232   310.836.3939   fax 310.836.3980

236

1

2

3

5

6

1.-2. Details of marquee at Denver Performing Arts Complex.
3.-4. Sculptural details at Citadel Corporate Park.
5.-6. Identity and signage for a shop.

VRONTIKIS DESIGN OFFICE

VRONTIKIS DESIGN OFFICE

"I respond to each project individually," says Petrula Vrontikis, principal and creative director of her own design firm. "I pride myself on giving clients something no one else can--innovative design solutions specifically tailored to their needs." Her client base encompasses a wide spectrum--from E! Entertainment Television to Children's Hospital to several Los Angeles and Tokyo restaurants.

Vrontikis Design Office handles a range of projects including brochures, identity programs, press kits, annual reports, special events promotions and on-air graphics. "I don't like to push style on clients," says Petrula. "I don't think that's my role as a graphic designer. My role is to find solutions that are appropriate yet very progressive."

Petrula, who has taught the advanced graphic design studies course at Art Center since 1989, enjoys the business side of design, as well. "I love working with people and helping their businesses grow and promoting their products and services. When you really take the time to understand what a company is doing and how your work relates to their big picture, you get long term accounts as opposed to short term projects."

1

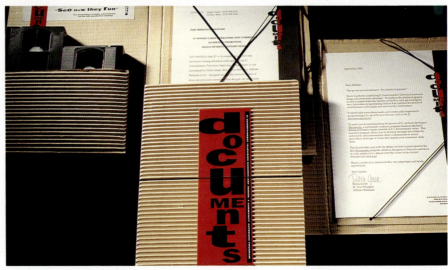

2

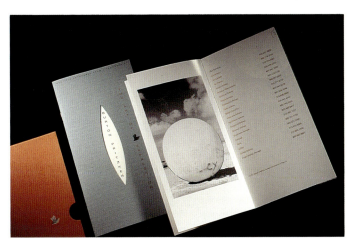

3

6

4

7

5

1. Marketing materials for E! Entertainment Television.
2. An E! community outreach program, packaging.
3.-7. Direct mail promotions for a printer featuring the work of various photographers.

1

2

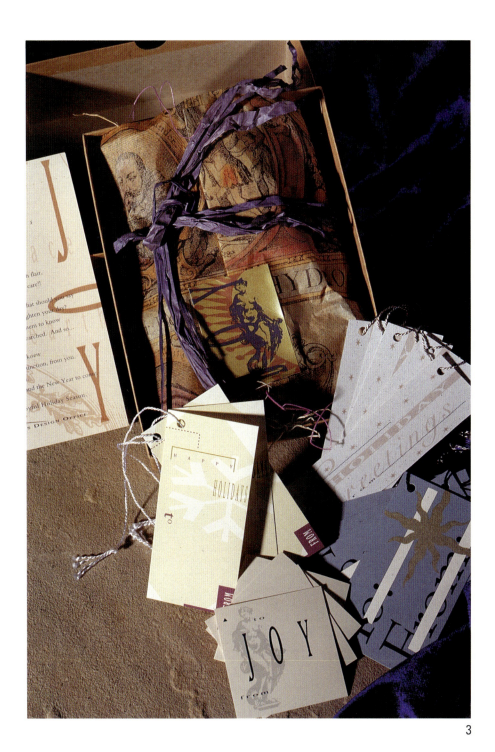

3

4

1. Restaurant promotional materials.
2. Detail.
3. Studio holiday promotion containing an assortment of gift tags.
4. Stationery system and fund raising brochure for the Paloma Society.

VRONTIKIS DESIGN OFFICE

2

1

1. Brochure for child care services
2. A brochure explaining fertility programs.
3. Service brochures for a regional medical center.
4. Prospectus outlining the pediatric residency program at Childrens Hospital.
5. Symbol for an agency that represents storyboard artists.
6. Symbol for a real estate management consulting firm.
7. Logo for a marketing firm.
8. Logo for a public relations firm.
9. Patient information brochure.
10. Capabilities brochure for the Motion Picture and Television Fund.

3

4

5

6

7

8

9

10

VRONTIKIS DESIGN OFFICE

2021 Pontius Avenue   Los Angeles, CA 90025   310.478.4775   fax 310.478.4685

1. Annual report and seminar catalogs for the MacNeal-Schwendler Corporation.
2.-3. Annual report for Arco Foundation.
4. Software documentation brochures.

THE WARREN GROUP

THE WARREN GROUP

Illustration pervades Linda Warren's work, giving it a witty, editorial style. With an emphasis on specialty brochures and one-time projects, Warren and her staff have designed capabilities pieces, brochures, and annual reports for a range of clients including Mattel, the South Coast Air Quality Management District, Allergan, Inc., St. Vincent Medical Center and Harvard-Westlake School.

A graduate of Occidental College, the designer majored in English and minored in art. Her studio, which she opened in 1984, is located in Venice.

The firm aims for creative that is unique. Warren says, "We search continually for illustrators and photographers whose work is original. To me, a piece is successful when everyone's efforts blend and work together as a whole."

1

2

3

4

5

1. Kimberly Hillman and Linda Warren.
2. Studio holiday "Adam & Eve" promotion.
3. The studio with Phoebe.
4. Catalog for Harvard-Westlake School.
5. Birth announcement booklet.

THE WARREN GROUP

248

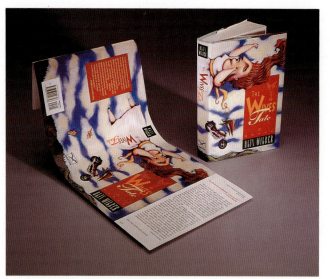

1

3

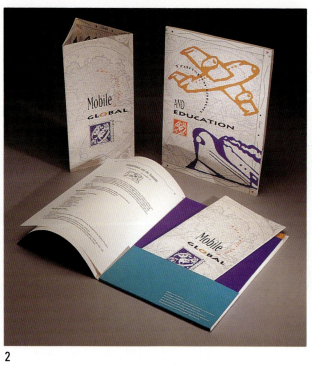

2

4

1. Book jacket for Norton Books.
2. Education program for Orange County Transportation Authority
3. Quarterly publication for a healthcare provider.
4. Brochure for the Air Quality Management District, AQMD.
5. Promotional brochure for a photographer.
6. Smog education poster for the AQMD.

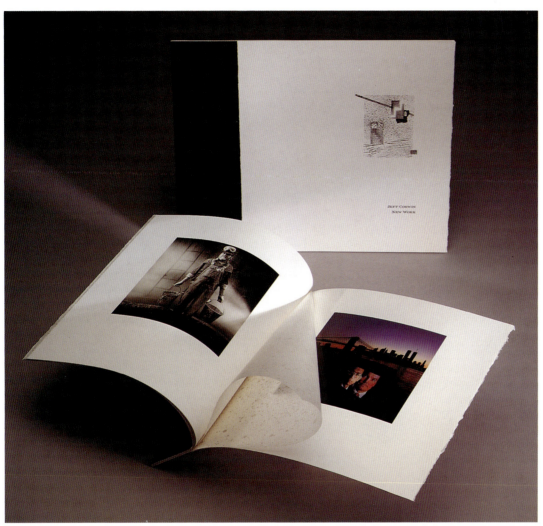

THE WARREN GROUP

250

1

4

7

2

5

8

3

6

9

10

11

1. Logo for Aids Project Los Angeles education program.
2. Symbol for Orange County Transportation Authority education program.
3. Symbol for an Air Quality Management District educational campaign.
4. Logo for the UCLA School of Theater, Film and Television newsletter.
5. Symbol for an Italian restaurant.
6. Logo for Team Effort sports clothing.
7. Logo for a USC programming language research project.
8. Logo for a clothing manufacturer.
9. Press kit and collateral for an AQMD educational program.
10. Award booklet honoring Mattel employees.
11. Promotional brochure for a photographer.

THE WARREN GROUP

622 Hampton Drive   Venice, CA 90291   310.396.6316   fax 310.396.1265

1

2

1. Advertisements for a printer.
2. Marketing materials for Anaheim Memorial Hospital.
3. Annual report for St. Vincent Medical Center.

3

WHITE DESIGN

WHITE DESIGN

"A lot of what's out there is designed to satisfy the designer's needs rather than the client's," comments John White, principal and creative director of White Design. "I approach design from a business perspective. Understanding the way businesses work is essential in creating effective communications."

The Long Beach-based firm, which was founded in 1989, develops annual reports, brochures, posters, corporate identity programs, stationery systems and exhibit design. White says, "We recently completed an exhibit design for Disney's upcoming Westcot Center. This was a welcome opportunity for us, as we had only one exhibit in our portfolio at the time."

A graduate of Art Center, John works with his design team to develop conceptual ideas that are marketing-driven. He says." We really try and dig through and get to the essence of the problem, which becomes the foundation of our idea. This philosophy has contributed to our continued, steady growth."

1

2 3

1. The White Design staff, Susan Garland Foti, John White, Chaunte' Kashiwa, Aram Youssefian and Amy White.
2.-4. Studio holiday greeting cards, t-shirts and chocolate logo promotions.
5. Yellow pages marketing brochure for an advertising agency.
6. Logo and stationery for Espia Corporation.
7. Poster/brochure for the city of Brea.

4

5

6

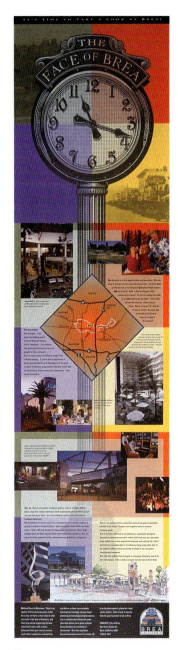
7

1

2

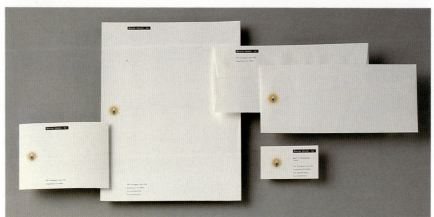

3

1.-3. Symbol, capabilities brochure, collateral material and stationery for Beacon Energy, Inc.
4. Annual report for Applied Magnetics, Inc.
5. Annual report for Metrobank.
6. Symbol for Commons Restaurant.
7. Logo for a restaurant.
8. Promotional logo for The Prudential, a sponsor of the America's Cup.
9. Promotional logo for the City of Brea for the construction on Imperial Highway.
10. Logo for Pacific Coast Financial Securities.

WHITE DESIGN

4

5

6

7

8

9

10

WHITE DESIGN

1

2

3

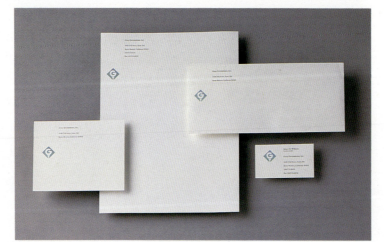

4

5

6

7

1. Exhibit for the new addition to The Farmer's Market.
2.-3. Exhibit for an addition to Disneyland theme park.
4.-5. Symbol and stationery application for Golf Enterprises, Inc.
6. Capabilities brochure for a law firm.
7. Capabilities brochure for a real estate brokerage firm.

WHITE DESIGN

4500 E. Pacific Coast Highway   Suite 320   Long Beach, CA 90804   310.597.7772   fax 310.494.5151

1

2

4

3

1. Promotional event logo.
2.-3. The Wine Auction party.
4. Collateral materials for the event.

INDEX

INDEX

Kimberly Baer Design Associates
620 Hampton Drive
Venice Ca 90291
310.399.3295
fax 310.399.7964

Baker Design Associates
1450 20th Street
Santa Monica CA 90404
310.453.6613
fax 310.453.4015

Bass Yager & Associates
7039 W. Sunset Bloulevard
Los Angeles CA 90038
213.466.9701
fax 213.466.9700

Besser Joseph Partners
1546 7th Street Suite 301
Santa Monica CA 90401
310.458.1899
fax 310.394.1789

Bright & Associates
901 Washington Boulevard
Venice CA 90291
310.450.2488
fax 310.452.1613

Michael Brock Design
8075 W. 3rd Street #300
Los Angeles CA 90048
213.932.0283
fax 213.932.8165

Margo Chase Design
2255 Bancroft Avenue
Los Angeles CA 90039
213.668.1055
fax 213.668.2470

COY Los Angeles
9520 Jefferson Boulevard
Culver City CA 90232
310.837.0173
fax 310.559.1706

Curry Design
1501 Main Street
Venice CA 90291
310.399.4626
fax 310.399.8524

The Designory, Inc.
211 E. Ocean Boulevard
Long Beach CA 90802
310.432.5707
fax 310.491.0140

Rod Dyer Group
8360 Melrose Avenue
Los Angeles CA 90069
213.655.1800
fax 213.655.9159

Stan Evenson Design, Inc.
4445 Overland Avenue
Culver City CA 90230
310.204.1995
fax 310.204.4879

The Graphics Studio
811 N. Highland Avenue
Los Angeles CA 90038
213.466.2666
fax 213.466.5685

April Greiman, Inc.
620 Moulton Street #211
Los Angeles CA 90031
213.227.1222
fax 213.227.8651

Hard Werken
5514 Wilshire Boulevard
9th Floor
Los Angeles CA 90029
213. 913.0406
fax 213.913.3433

Wayne Hunt Design, Inc.
87 N. Raymond Avenue #215
Pasadena CA 91103
818.793.7847
fax 818.793.2549

Looking
660 South Avenue 21
Los Angeles CA 90031
213.226.1086
fax 213.222.9170

Louey/Rubino Design Group
2525 Main Street #204
Santa Monica CA 90405
310.396.7724
fax 310.396.1686

Maddocks & Company
2011 Pontius Avenue
Los Angeles CA 90025
310.477.4227
fax 310.479.5767

Norman Moore/Design Art, Inc.
6311 Romaine #7311
Los Angeles CA 90038
213.467.2984
fax 213.467.1985

Ph.D
1524A Cloverfield Boulevard
Santa Monica CA 90404
310.829.0900
fax 310.829.1859

Sargent & Berman
1237A Third Street
Santa Monica CA 90401
310.576.1070
fax 310.576.1074

Shiffman Young Design Group
7421 Beverly Boulevard #4
Los Angeles CA 90036
213.930.1816
fax 213.930.1056

Shimokochi/Reeves
4465 Wilshire Boulevard
Los Angeles CA 90010
213.937.3414
fax 213.937.3417

Siegel & Gale/Cross
3465 W. 6th Street #300
Los Angeles CA 90020
213.389.1010
fax 213.389.0064

Patrick SooHoo Designers
8800 Venice Boulevard
Mezzanine A
Los Angeles CA 90034
310.836.8800
fax 310.839.3039

SoS:Los Angeles
3359 Garden Avenue
Studio 1
Los Angeles CA 90039
213.660.4588
fax 213.660.3247

Sussman/Prejza & Co, Inc.
3960 Ince Boulevard
Culver City CA 90232
310.836.3939
fax 310.836.3980

Vrontikis Design Office
2021 Pontius Avenue
Los Angeles CA 90025
310.478.4775
fax 310.478.4685

The Warren Group
622 Hampton Drive
Venice CA 90291
310.396.6316
fax 310.396.1265

White Design
4500 E. Pacific Coast Highway
#320
Long Beach CA 90804
310.597.7772
fax 310.494.5151

264

This book would not have been possible without those who contributed the impressive selection of work shown here.

I would specially like to thank Jim Cross for his essay and Eric Myer whose photographs illustrate the beginning of the book., as well as all those who put their efforts into providing me with the information needed to produce Los Angeles: Graphic Design.

Among those who deserve particular recognition for their contribution are Anita Bennett, Paul Jager and Lisa Woodard for their production assistance.